S A N A N D A

THIS REPRODUCTION
IS AN ACTUAL
PHOTOGRAPH TAKEN
ON JUNE 1st, 1961, IN
CHICHEN ITZA,
YUCATAN, BY
DR. STEINBECK,
ONE OF THIRTY
ARCHAEOLOGISTS
WORKING IN THE
AREA AT THAT TIME.

SANANDA APPEARED
IN A VISIBLE,
TANGIBLE BODY
AND PERMITTED
HIS PHOTOGRAPH
TO BE TAKEN.

"BY THE GRACE OF THE GREAT COMMANDER
SHALL THEY BE MADE TO SEE THE
GLORY OF THE HEAVENS"

Recorded by Sister Thedra

—SANANDA

CELESTIAL RAISE

'Tiers of Light'
Pouring Fourth From The Son

Celestial Raise

'Tiers of Light'

Pouring Fourth From The Son

Compiled by
Marcus

Published 1986
A.S.S.K.
P.O. Box 35
Mt. Shasta, CA 96067

Printed by Naturegraph Publishers, Inc., Happy Camp, California.

Council
Table of Contents

Chapter Five

Governments of the World—or—

To Govern Within The Eternal I AM

Chapter Six

Change, Preparation, Survival, and Victory

About The Photographs

"Interspersed throughout the previous chapters of messages are 43 of the most unique and wonder-full photographs. All of the photos except: "spaceship with the Blue Angels;" "Mother Eternal;" "Baja California 'cloud'; " and "The Eagle"—were taken around the Mt. Shasta Area.

Shasta is a towering volcanic mountain in the northern-most region of California, rising over 14,000 feet. This beloved portion of Mother Earth in its awe inspiring beauty, has long been known and sought after for the energy so often expressed as being spiritual and uplifting. The gifts of this area, as shown in the expressions in this book, is one of an obvious acknowledgement of the purity of the atmosphere to a degree bearable to those who can use this as a transformation point from other dimensions.

I have watched these wondrous energy exchanges between higher (more evolved) dimensions, and have over and over been exhilarated by the wonders of these "so called clouds." Even before they make visible physical appearance possible "I can feel the energies and know that they have stepped down to be close to us." I have watched these patterns take on form, change within minutes and fractions of minutes. Coming at times in vast contrast with "nature formed clouds," and other times as "A Master of the Elements leaving suddenly with no trace to be found."

—Marcus

Index Of Speakers

The following list is an acknowledgement of appreciation and reference, to the Beings and the Source of All Being, for the messages given in this book:

1. White Star
2. Joshua
3. Sananda
4. Archangel Gabriel
5. Stephani
6. Theoaphylos
7. Monka
8. Andromeda Rex
9. Ramtha
10. Starla
11. Hatonn
12. Zanadar
13. Archangel Michael
14. Ashtar
15. Djwal Kul
16. Sanat Kumara
17. Lord Kuthumi
18. Yogunda
19. Maitreya
20. Mother Eternal (Sarah)
21. Captain Zoa
22. Krona
23. 'D'
24. Marius
25. Masters of Korendor
26. Berean
27. Matton
28. Aleva
29. Surnia of Mars and K.O.R.
30. Christmon
31. Apollo
32. Captain Arma
33. Caladar Ramonsara
34. Jycondria
35. Yada
36. Bor
37. Aljanon
38. Alon
39. El Morya
40. Cuptan Fetogia
41. Xyletron
42. Sonic
43. Kwan Yin
44. Captain Arcturus
45. Raymere
46. Hilarion
47. Silver Ray
48. Beatrix
49. Korton
50. Mary
51. The Father Solen Aum Solen
52. Archangel Uriel
53. Archangel Zadkiel
54. Archangel Raphael
55. Archangel Jophiel
56. Archangel Chamuel

Index of Channels

Name	Affiliated Light Center	Location
Sister Thedra	Ass. of Sananda & Sanat Kumara	Mt. Shasta, CA
Tuella	Guardian Action Publications	Durango, CO
Tuieta	Portals of Light	Ft. Wayne, IN
J.Z. Knight	Ramtha Dialogues	Yelm, WA
KaRene & Omar	Gateway Newsletter	Norman, OK
Carol Hall	Galacticom	Menlo Park, CA
Jon Fox	Hilarion	San Rafael, CA
Ann Valentin	S.E.E.	Sunnyvale, CA
Lyara	Golden Rays Center	Phoenix, AZ
Bluebird	Universarius	Taylor, AZ
Joan Brown		England
Trevor James		
Lucy Colson		
Sarah Gran		
Bob Graham		
Bonnie Ireland		
George W. Van Tassel		

Index of Photographers

Kevin Lahey	Kevin Lahey Photography	P.O. Box 650, Mt. Shasta
Michael Radford	Mt. Shasta Crystal & Gem	P.O. Box 389, Mt. Shasta
Zenon Michalak	Aurora Studios	P.O. Box 876, Mt. Shasta
Michael Zanger	Shasta Mountain Guides	1938 W. Hill Rd., Mt. Shasta
W. & J. Everett		4929 Rancho Grande, Del Mar, California
Marcus	Celestial Raise Productions	P.O. Box 625, Mt. Shasta
Sister Thedra	A.S.S.K.	P.O. Box 35, Mt. Shasta

Index of Publications & Books
Through Which the Compilation of This Book was Possible

A.S.S.K. Scripts	The 'Sibors Portions'	Sister Thedra
A Call to Arms	A.S.S.K. Newsletter	Various Channels
Universal Network	Guardian Action Newsletter	Tuella
Portals of Light	Channeled Newsletter	Tuieta
Ramtha Dialogues	Audio & Video Tapes	J.Z. Knight
Gateways	Newsletter	KaRene & Omar
Aquarian Quest	Newsbooklet	Carol Hall
Hilarion	Tapes	Jon Fox
New Age Teachings	Newsletter	
The Universalian	Newsletter	
Voice of Universarius	Newsbooklet	
Axminster Light Center	Newsletter	
Lightlines	Newsletter	
ASHTAR 'A Tribute'	Book	Tuella
Messages for the Coming Decade	Book	Tuella
Project: World Evacuation	Book	Tuella
The Dynamics of Cosmic Telepathy	Book	Tuella
Letters from Home #1	Book	Tuieta
Letters from Home #2	Book	Tuieta
Letters from Home #3	Book	Tuieta
Messages of Light	Book	Joan Brown

Inner Art Design by Nadine Aiello of 'Alone Productions

DEDICATION

This book is dedicated to

The FATHER WithIN

For without HIS Presence Within

ALL factors INvolved

This expression of His Love

Would have still been a thought

Awaiting His Children of Light

To Bring it INto manifestation

FOR WE ARE HIS MANifestation

Of L O V E

INTRODUCTION

Heavenly Signs

I greet the myriad *stars* in the *silent night,*
　All *signs* of the *greatness* of *His love* . . .
And my heart leaps with *joy,* as a streaking *light,*
　Signals a response from above.

Oh *silent night,* oh *holy night,*
　The heavens *proclaim His Glory*
How blind the eye, how blind the mind,
　That knows not the *heavenly story.*

He comes in the *clouds,* he comes in the *sky,*
　To those with an eye to *see,*
With an ear to *hear,* the *call* rings clear . . .
　"I have come to set you *free.*"

Oh, yes, there's a *star* in the *heavenly night,*
　A *cloud* in the *heavenly day*
Angel music to greet the *soul* . . .
　And *guide* it on it's *way.*

Oh blest is he with eyes that *see,*
　And ears that *hear His story,*
Blest is the *soul* that follows the *light,*
　And finds it's *home in glory.*

Teska/Deska   **—White Star**

Clouds of Heaven

"And I might add that before this generation is through, you will observe the greatest celestial activity ever witnessed on this planet, as these so called 'clouds of heaven,' which are merely a condensation of those vehicles, arrive in great numbers and defy your wind as they remain or oppose it. That is why it is mentioned that Christ's return shall be on the clouds of heaven. They are the vehicles, when fully materialized, are great gleaming, metallic, crystalline vehicles used in the great enormous outreaches of the celestial realms."

Received by Bob Graham   **—Joshua**

"Ye See The Cloud Yet Ye See Me Not"

"Sori, Sori—I am come yea, I am Come—hear ye that which I say unto thee, I am present—yet many there be asking of others—what think ye? Is it not written that He cometh in a cloud? Yea, it is so written—ye know not that which is written—while ye wait ye see not—ye ask of others—ye poor in spirit, which know me not—while ye have slept on thine feet I have come, yea, Mine sleeping ones I say awaken All ye that sleep—I am Come even as it is written, even in a cloud. Ye see the cloud yet ye see me not, for the cloud be within thee—I say look up—see that which I say unto thee shall be made clear when ye accept Me as I am—for that which I am. Know ye that which I say unto thee this day?"

Recorded by Sister Thedra   **—Sananda**

Association of Sananda & Sanat Kumara

Interspersed throughout this book are quotes taken from the communications or teachings referred to as the "Scripts" through the channel known as Sister Thedra. Sister Thedra has been chosen by The Lord God Sananda (the one who walked the Earth as the Master Jesus—and who is known to our beloved Guardians on the space craft as the "Commander-in-Chief") to introduce the new name of Sananda and the teachings of the illumined beings who represent the Great White Brotherhood (see the message "The White Brotherhood"). These who work through such as this one (Sister Thedra) to reach and assist mankind, have come through the Love that they feel for all mankind, in this hour of Great Change and man's need for knowledge and awareness. Sister Thedra is in communication daily with Sananda and the other Elder Brothers. These teachings in the form of scripts and also the newsletter "A Call to Arms" together number thousands of pages and are available by writing to:

Association of Sananda & Sanat Kumara
P.O. Box 35
Mt. Shasta, California 96067

"A New Cycle Beginning"

"Sori, Sori—It is Mine time to speak of things to come, and it shall be as nothing before—for it is given unto Me to see the records of events—and it is said, We tell time by the Great events—and no event takes place without it's cause. When the effect is seen or come about, we see it as done, or finished—a new cycle beginning. And it is now come when one cycle endeth and another beginneth. This one just ended, is but the intermediate with which ye of Earth are concerned, for thy time extendeth yet into the beginning of the new and larger cycle of time."
Recorded by Sister Thedra   **—Sananda**

"The Same Star Ship Which Stood Guard Over Bethlehem"

"Beloved of Earth: Hear ye Me from afar, for I am in the 'Star Ship' whereupon I have spent much time; and whereupon I am prepared to receive them which are to be brot within this place—the same Star Ship which stood guard over Bethlehem on the night on which the One and Only Sananda was born unto Mother Mary. It was I Gabriel, which came unto her, as I now come unto another which is prepared to receive of The Father and of the Holy Ghost."
—Archangel Gabriel

"The XTX Did Monitor and Stand Guard Upon the Horizon"

"And I say we of the XTX stood guard as the Star Ship did stand guard upon the Horizon that night and day of Sananda's birth (as Jesus). I say that the XTX did monitor and stand guard upon the horizon that night which shall live within the heart of each one which stood upon the Holy ground which has been dedicated to Truth and Justice."
Recorded by Sister Thedra   **—Stephani**

Guardian Action Publications

Interspersed throughout this book are quotes taken from the book ASHTAR—A Tribute. *This book was compiled by Tuella, and also are the messages channeled from her presented within. Other books that have been made possible through and by her efforts are:* Project World Evacuation, The Master Symbol of the Solar Cross, World Messages for the Coming Decade, The Dynamics of Cosmic Telepathy, *and also available is the quarterly newletter entitled* Universal Network. *These publications and others are available, for information write to:*

Guardian Action Publications
P.O. Box 2566
Durango, Colorado 81302

"The Voices of These Who Come From Other Worlds"

"So, I shall call unto those who follow Me, to listen to the voices of these who come from other worlds, and harden not your hearts against their words nor practices. Rather, lift up Love unto them and desire for their coming, for *they are the angels of the the harvest!*"
Received by Tuella   **—I Am Sananda**

"Return of Herald Angels"

"Ashtar is of the herald angels and first manifested in the early '50's through so-called UFO type of communication with individuals like George van Tassel and others, awaiting the return of herald angels, who are the participants in the so-called UFO's that have manifested from time to time. They are observing from their sphere (which is not physical) the actions of men and nations as the periods of time ripen for the return of the Christ, who will return on those same clouds of heaven, which are partial of full materializations of the vehicles used in the celestial realms."
Received by Bob Graham   **—Joshua**

Interdimensional Fellowship— Interplanetary Coexistence

"They (man) shall rub shoulders with those whom they have called the 'angels', yet whom they have come to know as brothers from other worlds. The blessings of interdimensional fellowship, and interplanetary coexistence will lead into heights of glory so long prepared for it."
Received by Tuella   **—Jesus the Christ**

"For I AM The Householder Who Cometh"

"These come as My Angels, to reap that which has been sown, to divide and set asunder the tares from the wheat, to gather the wheat into My Barn. For I AM the householder who cometh at the end of the day for an account from His Servants, and to give to all men justly in the manner given by them to Me."
Received by Tuella   **I AM Sananda**

Portals of Light

Interspered thoroughout this book are quotes taken from the communications known as "The Portals of Light," thru the channel Tuieta. Tuieta as with the previous sisters mentioned (Thedra, Tuella) works with our Beloved Guardians, the Masters, the Archangels, that which is known as The Great White Brotherhood. She is very active in this work of receiving messages, and with these she has put them together into books. The ones available at this time are Letters From Home, Volumes 1, 2, and 3; The Prophet, and transcriptions of the weekly messages are also available. For information on how to receive any of these write to:

Portals of Light
P.O. Box 5731
Ft. Wayne, Indiana 46895

"You Will See All Ones of Light"

"You have come to do a most glorious thing. You have come to be on this planet. I can speak of this with a measure of knowing for you see I have walked of this planet. I walked of this planet many times. But I learned as I walked. And it is now, that I walk of this planet no more. For I have learned of that which I had come to learn, and I did that which I had come to do. And now I am of a dimension that is not seen by your out turned eye at this hour. Please notice beautiful ones, I say this hour. For the hour shall approach when you will see me, as you will see all ones of Light. And oh how glorious shall be our reunion, as your eye is tuned to behold our vision."

—Theoaphylos

"It Is Vital That You Look Beyond"

"This shall also be a season when there shall be some sightings of our shuttle ships, and these reports will be filtering back to you. Indeed some of you may have the opportunity to see these yourselves. I would say to you each one, it is vital that you look beyond, that you feel, that you know we come in love, we come in service of our Lord Sananda, our Commander-in-Chief. We do not come to amuse, we do not come to entertain and those that would ask this of you I would ask that ye set their record straight. Our Lord Sananda and the Hierarchial Board have determined what will be for ye ones of Earth. We follow his divine instruction. Know we come in peace and love. Know we are Not A Phenomena.

—Monka

"To Raise Your Vibratory Rate"

"We shall accelerate the energies that are coming to the Light workers now as never before. We shall, in every way possibly permitted, by Law, help you ones of Earth to raise your vibratory rate. We shall begin to engage many of you in meditational or nocturnal experiences that we give you full awareness of future events, events that have already taken place on the etheric plane. We shall also bring more of you to our ships, and allow you to have recall of the experience as a way of preparing you for your lift-off."
Received by Tuieta   **Andromeda Rex**

Ramtha Dialogues

Below and interspersed throughout this book are portions transcribed from the tapes recorded by "Ramtha Dialogues." The channel, a most dedicated woman, J.Z. Knight, allows the wondrous teacher Ramtha to come through and totally animate and use the whole of her body. The Dialogues consist of a period of teaching to an audience, some (the intensives) occur from 2 to 3 days, others (the retreats) are for a period of 7 days. These dialogues are growing rapidly in attendance as the persons who have experienced them share their appreciation with others, of the en-light-enment that does occur through such an interaction. There are available video tapes, audio tapes, and books transcribed from previous Dialogues. To receive a list of these of dates for scheduled Dialogues write to:

Ramtha Dialogues
P.O. Box 1210
Yelm, Washington 98597

This work is based, in part, upon Ramtha Dialogues® *a series of magnetic recordings authored by J.Z. Knight, with her permission. Ramtha ® is a trademark registered with the U.S. patent and trademark office.*

Note: This particular cloud pattern chose to defy the wind and remain, staying in one position for four days without movement. ➧

"There is Life Everywhere"

"There is another group of brothers that come from what is called star travels in your time, they come from what is termed galaxies as they are known and seen. There is life, master*, in other places—never be so pious in your thinking or pompous in your thinking rather, to be that you are the only ones who live in the only place allotted for life, there is life everywhere. Entities that travel through time and space as it were, their journeys are more arduous than those that come from within the core**. Their time is time for they have not learned to master dimensional travel, thus they purport themselves through space as it is seen and known in it's dimensional frame through the propulsion that is called 'light,' the propulsion that is called light, is the closest thing to perfected energy, master*, and they utilize it to travel upon. Light projected into a void creates what is called a highway of sorts to travel upon—a projectile using light will be an energy that this place will soon learn of, and already are in the manufacture of.

They come from places that you term in your time as what is called galaxies, star systems as they are known, there is a place that is called Alpha Centuri, there is a great civilization there upon it, and what be their mission unto Terra***—to explore, to find the life that exists upon this plane and its cultures, when one as it were indeed goes into another adventure master, they go into the adventure to see all that lies beyond their expected realms whatever they may conclude. Entities that come from other galaxies are explorers, they are adventurers and this is their frontier—and what think they of us indeed, they think, master*, that we be primitive in

(* master—a term Ramtha uses to greet people; ** the core is the inner Earth; ***Terra is another term used for Earth)

PHOTO BY SISTER THEDRA

our creativeness—but understand that even in their history all their peoples have gone through such times as it is seen.

There is a brinking point of time and its change upon this plane—that the higher realizations that are spoken of are not only for this place but for *all places*. Thought is wherever *God is,* and wherever God *is all life is.* The higher realizations are projected by *Masters,* of Love and Peace and a granduence of Light, it is the Light that they will see. And upon the turn of this time as it is so seen in New Ages, master*, there will be a *great hope* come from that which is termed the Galaxies, there will be a union of spirits, master*—for they see and *live* on *light* and we are beginning only to think of it. *There will be a union of sorts to be sure.* Their realization is a Truth. The color of their propulsions is called light blue in it's color, and have no darker colors for their propulsion is needed for long distances. Blue be a higher color of perfection, white being no travel but complete travel, and this is a mystery in your mind.''
Channeled by J.Z. Knight   **—Ramtha**

"The Door That Unlocks the Kingdom, It Is On Your Side !!!"

''Masters do not unfold in that which is called 'schools', that which is called hideaways where they all come together so to speak, they do not unfold there. They unfold individually. No one in this wondrous, powerful, august body can unfold your knowingness not even Me. I AM bold enough to tell you that. I AM an All Powerful God. I AM at the epic of that which I AM, but that which I AM is not greater than that which you are, the only difference is: I know—lived and became the Lord God of My Being. And that to which I come from is the totality called forever. You have to come to that understanding for not even I could force you to know. No teacher can. Social consciousness is where sheep herd. And where the leader is not one but the collective group who have designed their destinies. You possess the power to manifest, and do, but the door that unlocks the Kingdom, it is on your side!!! *Now!,* what is interesting here for you to understand, you are only going to know and allow as much as *you want to.* You are only going to unfold to the measure that *you want to.* You are only going to embrace this knowingness to the measure that *you want to.* Remember whatever you do with it, it is a dream. Until you come to the reality called God it always will be. Becoming unfolding Masters are an awakening mankind. They awake from slumber of the games and the dreams. There are those of you who will not allow this full process to unfold. Why? many many reasons. But that which is important to the collective is: That you will be ashamed to live that which is called your individual truth, to an uncertain world. You will be intimidated to think on your own. It is a great step to be different and yet difference *is you,* the same is collective consciousness. Remember we only spoke in the history of your times of what it takes to be a genius, it only means to be you rather than the whole, the whole as sheep they are without identity, you see? They go to heaven or hell, they are without identity. They are a limited faction. Those who will be ashamed to live their truth, can not in their understanding at this point allow to let go of judgement. It is important to criticize their brothers. It is important for them to be critical, for you see they have not learned the steadfastness of loving who they are without *comparison to the others.''*
Channeled by J.Z. Knight   **—Ramtha**

"By His Own Hand Shall He Open All The Doors"

"And blest is the man which can be his own carter and say: 'Thy will be done: I am as thou art, and I am not of the Earth, yet I am in it.' And he shall see the glory of the dawn: for it is given unto him to know wherein is his strength. And not a place shall he seek to hide, but he shall go forth to meet that which apportioned unto Him. And he shall know the truth and it shall make him free. And not a person shall set foot against his door. And not a person shall keep him out of the Father's house, for by his own hand shall he open all the doors which have been closed unto him."

Recorded by Sister Thedra **—Sananda**

"Being Raised to the Awareness of the Changes"

"More and more the consciousness of multitudes of Earth Beings is being raised to the awareness of the changes occurring on that planet this very day. Persons are coming into the knowing of their 'lighted' origins and their reason for being on that planet at this time. Butterflies are continually getting closer to that day of realization when they shall emerge from that cloak of veiled Earth awareness, that cocoon of limited vision, and spread their wings in the sunshine of a greatly changed planet, a planet of high vibratory rate and corresponding enlightenment.

This present hour of Earth change shall be the culmination of literally thousands of years effort on the part of the 'Lighted' beings throughout the universe to bring enlightenment to that rather dark little planet. Those of you who read these words are most apt to be there to see these great changes come about. These changes have been prophesized for centuries, and now at last we can assure you that they are about to be realized in your lifetime.

Sound like a pipedream? Then so be it. The fact remains, however, that there are thousands of persons on Earth right now who know from within their beings that this metamorphosis of planet Earth truly is about to become your reality. Such is the awareness of persons who have spent much of their current lives getting in touch with vibrations and thought from realms far from the reaches of Earth environment."

Received by Robert McCampbell **—Starla**

"Manifest the Teachings"

"You can't instill want into another God, you can only manifest the teachings and when they're ready—when they are ready they will become."

Channeled by J.Z. Knight **—Ramtha**

"Souls that are in Communion with Other Ones"

"And then there are other ones on Earth who have evolved thru previous embodiments to be Souls that are in communion with other ones. These ones might agree prior to embodiment to allowing their vehicles to be used by another. At such time, there is a conscious agreement between the one of the dimension that is unseen by you and the one who is in embodiment to exchange places for a brief period of time to accomplish specific activities at that particular time. For example, you have seen of that one that Lord Ramtha comes through. You have seen that he comes through and completely overtakes this body. He uses this particular vehicle for a period of time. The soul that normally resides within that

vehicle goes forth into another dimension and stays there until such time as he bids that they might return to this body. Other ones of your earthly place do the same. They have agreed to let these vehicles in which they reside be used by various ones, by Lords of the Universe, of ones that you know as Masters, as ones that you know as brothers of space."
Received by Tuieta — **Hatonn**

"When Ye So Love Each Other"

"I shall give you a *'portion'* yet I shall give many others a *'portion'* and when ye so love each other that ye put them on the table together ye will begin to see the Divine Plan . . . This is *my banyan tree,* and it shall put down roots in every country of the Earth."
Recorded by Sister Thedra — **Sananda**

"Great Love, Great Joy, Great Merriment is Within You"

"Create with your thots, and be your thots. Manifest all that does come. Great beauty do you have locked within your sleeping vessel. Great love, great joy, great merriment is within you. But you see you have been taught in order to come to the alter of the Everliving God you must come with a downed countenance, and you must crawl upon your knees and you must speak of your unworthiness. And this has been given to you, rote, after rote and rote. And you recognize if you have enough rote then you don't have to think. See you this? And I am saying take the rote and throw it away. Cut through it, and stand straight and stand tall before the altar of the Everliving God, and say to that which is the Lord God of Totality, "The Lord God of

my being recognizes that I am a manifestation of that which you are. Use of me that I might manifest that which you have sent me to do, that I might grow in mine own totality." And you say to me, "My brethren, this is heavy." And I say to you, "My brethren, tis so." For if you are as ones to think you have not the right to stand before the Lord God of Totality and proclaim who you are then indeed you are not ready to recognize who you are, and you are not ready to manifest that which you are capable of thinking."
Received by Tuieta — **Theoaphylos**

"And of course you don't have to !"

"Enlightenment is to be in knowledge of, that's what it means, to be in the knowingness, that is what a *master is.* Knowledge is that which challenges a closed mind to open. Knowledge is that which allows the mind to bloom—to allow the tenth to open up, so that miracles do exist, manifestations do exist.

And know you who the Glory of all that belongs, it is to your Beloved Father within you. Because it is the *Is* that you are. And His endowments are Life, Love, and Power. So when the grand things come forth in your life and the joy it is there speak to the *Father within you,* unto that which is called the Is, and give thanks and appreciation to God within. And the more that you do that the greater your God will shine forth. And when clouds seem to seep in the Light will dissolve them, understand? You begin to be in harmony with the life force if you do it. And of course you don't have to !

Of course you don't have to be happy. Of course you can stay where you are. Of course you don't even need to bring to your alter-ego's attention that a Divine personage self exists. You don't have to do that at all. It is not really required because

23

you haven't required it! So you can mish and mash and be confused, and unhappy, miserable wretched entities for the rest of this existence, I will pass you by. *It is your choice, it is your will that decides it.* And you shan't be judged, and you shan't not be loved, you are *always loved.* But know that when you have knowledge it gives you the insight and clarity and the reason for being. And it also rears forth that which is called personal self. The more you know, the better you will like yourself. The more that you understand your capabilities the more enticing you will become to you. And the little importance it will be to become so much for everyone else."

Channeled by J.Z. Knight   **—Ramtha**

The White Brotherhood

"Greetings in the White Light of Our Heavenly Father, I am Zanadar.

I extend to you my love and appreciation from realms of loving existence for all you do for the advancement for my home planet, Earth. I am Zanadar, elder of the Council for Human Awareness.

It is my extreme pleasure to be given the privilege of sharing with you information on the fraternity of advanced Earth souls known as The White Brotherhood.

There has been much commentary on the shortcomings of planet Earth as it is viewed by 'Lighted' beings from existences throughout the galaxies. It is true that we of Earth have an uphill struggle in our pursuit of universal understanding of love and harmonic existence, but little has been shared concerning the handicaps we encounter along our paths of awareness.

It is not my purpose to review with you the obstacles with which Earthbeings are confronted in their pursuit of awareness. It seems you are quite familiar with most of them. Likewise, it is not my purpose to point out all the beauties of our planet. If you do not acknowledge them, perhaps you just have not seen them.

Just what is The White Brotherhood?

First of all, white does not refer to racial skin tone. Our membership is composed of all Earth races and cultures. You might say we do not discriminate.

Brotherhood? Our Lord Jesus proclaimed his desire for love of all mankind during his ministry. A brotherhood is based on love and caring, and our organization works to enlarge it's membership of loving, caring beings in every way possible.

White is the color of purity. Purity in this instance refers to purity of thought, action and deed. Purity is a symbol not unlike clairty. Clarity can be described as a true perception of what is. A true perception is one which is unadulterated by foreign factors to its make-up. I would seem I could go on forever in this defining process. I do believe you have the necessary understanding.

At a given level of soul progression one reaches an awareness of what is pure thought, action and deed. When one does, we know we have a candidate for our brotherhood. Membership is optional, but most who qualify are pleased to 'sign on'. Dues are not high. One simply commits oneself to the betterment of mankind of Earth.

We are generous with life memberships. Each neophyte (beginner) receives one upon completion of his first mission. We are not sexist. Man and woman make up our organization.

We operate both in physical manifestation and in spirit. I make a distinction between spirit realms and etheric realms. The spirit realms to which I refer are primarily the operating grounds, so to speak, of The White Brotherhood while etheric realms are home to other beings of 'Light'.

PHOTO BY KEVIN LAHEY

The 'Light' and the White Light are essentially one and the same. It is all a matter of semantics.

Large numbers of our brotherhood are present on Earth as incarnates. They operate somewhat incognito except for those whose missions are to spread our word throughout the world. Who knows, you may be brushing elbows with us on your next trip to the grocery store.

The current Earth mission of enlightenment affords us the pleasure of working closely together with 'Lighted' beings from all over the universe. It does seem we do need help to bring Earth into levels of higher vibration within the allotted time of the Divine Plan.

It is most gratifying and impressive to welcome to our task the great numbers of 'Lighted' beings whose only interest in Earth is to bring it into 'Lighted' existence as a member of the Universal Confederation of Planets. We will be forever grateful to them.

The White Brotherhood has existed for what would seem to be eons of time, gradually increasing it's membership and scope of activities with the passage of time. It is possible for persons of Earth, who call this planet their home, to evolve in soul awareness to the point where they can actively work to help other humans along their path of awareness.

Much of the information that your channel has brought through to you has dealt with perceptions of Earth from extraterrestrial viewpoints. It is most interesting and helpful to ponder. It does tell it 'like it is' from the perspective of life in the universe, although some of you apparently feel it is too idealistic for current life of this planet.

As you may be aware, such communications, be they from space intelligences or from other 'Lighted' realms of existence, are designed to stretch your thinking and make you reach out for answers on your own. Without concerted effort on your part, your awareness unfoldment will proceed at a very leisurely rate. With conscious effort you can perceive *great changes* coming into your life. There are not free passes to awareness, as you may know, although most persons wish there were from time to time.

It is my purpose here to bring before you some insights to life of Earth from one who has been through it all, you might say. While not having experienced all the possible learnings of Earth life, I have tallied up a goodly number.

Our classroom, our planet, is not an easy one in which to live. The extremes of pleasure and distress are truly far apart, and they are dramatically pleasant on one hand and traumatically upsetting on the other. Then there is the big middle ground which brings its daily share of lessons to Earth inhabitants. Any way you cut the deck you are sure of turning up a learning lesson, be it large or small.

Of course, it is from the lessons of life that one puts distance behind oneself on the path of awareness.

With some five billion plus souls reaching out for awareness on Earth at this time, why is it that there seems to be no greater apparent effort toward enlightenment going on?

As stated before, we of The White Brotherhood and other 'Light' workers here work behind the scenes of Earth life. Our compatriots in physical existence work in areas of life which offer service to mankind. They pursue their tasks without special recognition from those around them, for they do not wear badges denoting speciality. They are guided by helpers in spirit, who channel help in various ways most often not perceived at the conscious level. In order to better accomplish their missions, they most often are not aware that they are on missions. It truly is a behind the scenes type of work we perform.

If some of us have reached high levels of awareness as Earth beings, why are there not more members of the White Brotherhood?

There are thousands of us who have achieved some measure of awareness as human beings, but the number is somewhat small compared with Earth's total population. Why?

Earth is an enigma to members of mankind throughout the universe. They do not understand how behavior as is manifested here can go on. Well, Earth is also somewhat an enigma even to those of us who call it our home. It is somewhat difficult, for example, for us to understand how so many of our fellow humans can carry on the way they do with behavior which can only be described as unenlightened.

One must remember that there are all stages of soul awareness on this planet. Very young souls share life on Earth with very old souls. Children are often excused for their actions because 'they didn't know better.' Well, in a sense, very young souls perhaps should be excused for their actions for the same reason. They are working through lessons of Kindergarten and first grade, so to speak.

Under the universal law of cause and effect, karma, souls need time to work out a balance in their soul existence. There are no mistakes in life, only actions and reactions. A soul, for instance, can spend a whole lifetime experiencing selfish greed, but then it may take another whole lifetime, perhaps more, to balance it out at a later time.

Even though a soul preplans** lifetime experiences before incarnating on Earth, once here the soul is unaware of such planning. If there is karma to be worked out from previous lifetimes, so shall it be, much to the consternation of the person involved. Thus karma can cause life to be perceived as violent, traumatic and unfair.

Lifetime after lifetime after lifetime human beings strive for advancement down the path of awareness, and lifetime after lifetime after lifetime they find themselves embroiled in karmic situations hindering such advancement.

What is happening on Earth in these times is that there is no more time left for human beings to resolve the imbalances of their soul existence on this planet. The grains of sand in the hour glass of Earth existence as an unenlightened planet have about all reached the bottom. *The planet is going to change,* and Earth souls are either going to have to raise the vibratory levels of their awareness to be compatible with the raising vibratory levels of the planet or they are going to have to depart the Earth. It is comforting to know that there is another planet ready and waiting for those who are to depart.

How has anyone in such an unenlightened atmosphere been able to advance one's awareness to a level of pure thought, action and deed?

Free will, my friends, is a condition which has always been present in man's existence. If one truly chooses to live a goodly life, a life which does not bring harm to others, a life of giving and sharing, one does not create karmic payback*** in one's existence. One does not need to be an old soul in order to exercise this option.

Then why do not all people of Earth strive for this good life?

Temptation, my friends, temptation.

Free will gives to each person the freedom of choice as to how to manage one's life. Each person is truly on a path of awareness of one's own choosing. Along that path are countless attractions which can alter the direction of life and offer meaningful experiences as well. Many of these attractions are perceived as most desirable, and thus they tempt the unaware person to try them out.

Life is meant to hold numerous experiences from which a person can learn, but it is not necessary to experience every

(** see message entitled "You Sign Your Contract")

(*** see message entitled "They Meet Their Contract")

possible situation of life in order to gain soul awareness. Those who choose many avenues will experience many avenues. It does not mean that they are any less special beings in the eyes of the Creator than anyone else. It just means that they have chosen to take more time with soul growth.

Those of us who achieve status of The White Brotherhood somehow have been inclined to bypass some of Earth's challenges which seem to tempt others. As I have said, it is not necessary to take on all of the challenges of Earth merely because they present themselves before you.

Likewise, the soul who seems to fall into the trap of temptation really isn't doing so at all. For one reason or another, that soul needs that particular experience. The word temptation has a rather negative connotation. That is because it has been associated with that which is 'immoral,' and also persons who appear to succumb to temptation often are perceived as having traumatic consequences as a result.

Temptation seems to imply wrongdoing. Truly there is no right or wrong in the universe. There are only one's perceptions of events.

This would seem to come into conflict with the Bible passage known as the Lord's prayer—'Lead us not into temptation.'

What Lord Jesus was trying to get across to his disciples, according to the gospel of St. Matthew, was that they should not stray from their task of pursuing righteousness if they were to attain the kingdom of God on Earth. He was, in fact, urging them to pursue the truth with firm resolve. Temptation, then, is the sidetracking of direction in pursuit of one's goals.

In summary, The White Brotherhood is a guiding force for persons of this planet who seek guidance and awareness of their greater truth. We work in both the physical and spiritual realms. We are not what you call etherics. We work with space intelligences and beings of etheric realms to bring enlightenment to our planet. The White Brotherhood symbol, the white cross within the white circle on a magenta background, is meant for protection for all enlightened beings working on Earth. All you need to do is send the thought, 'I invoke the symbol,' and we are there.

Our numbers are relatively small compared with the total Earth population, but our mission is large—to help as many members of the Earth community as possible make it into the New Age for Planet Earth.

We love this planet. It is a most beautiful sphere. We devote our entire existences to promoting its acceptance as a member planet of the Universal Confederation of Planets, that organization of 'Lighted' planets throughout the universe. It shall occur with the arrival of the New Age.

In the name of the Father, the Son and the Holy Ghost, I am Zanadar. Peace be with you.''
Channeled by Robert McCampbell   **Zanadar**

"You Sign Your Contract"

"This question of free will and predestination—it is a very good one, might I say. And it is easy to understand how there can be a measure of confusion. If you would—and here I shall use a very elementary earthly example—if you would for a moment picture yourself as you are seated before a barrister. And you are making a contract. And this contract you agree that you shall do this and this and this, and you shall not do this and this and this. And the barrister looks, and he says what about so and so? And this is added to the contract. And then you sign your contract. And as you use on earth, the stamp is placed upon this by your notary. And it is put on file, for this is your agreement, this is your contract.

29

And then you go forth from this hallowed place, and you are walking down the street. Part of your contract shall we say, as an example, is that you shall obey all traffic signs and all traffic regulations. And so as you leave of this, the halls of the barrister, and you go forth and you reach the end of your block. And there is a sign that flashes at you and it says *'Do not walk.'* Now you look to the right and there are no cars coming. And you look to the left and there are no cars coming. And the sign flashes *'Do not walk.'* And the sign flashes *'Do not walk.'* And you stand there for several moments and you say to yourself, 'There must be something wrong with this sign.' You have choice. Would you go against your agreement, for you have agreed that you would follow all of the traffic rules and regulations? Even though you feel the sign is not working properly would you go against this by using your choice? Or would you stand and would you wait until, according to your contract, it says, 'The sign flashes that you might walk across the intersection.'

You have choice. And let's say with your choice you choose to say, 'Forget it. I'm going to go across the street because I have better things to do than to wait here for a faulty sign.' So you go across the street. And about the time you get across the street—almost, a car comes around the corner very swiftly and *pop* you are in the next dimension. Now, if you had stayed and you obeyed your contract, that would not have happened, is this not so?

But you have choice. In all things you have choice because you are lord of your being. Because you are of the Divine Creator and you were given the ability to think, to have thought, to have reason. You were given this by the Divine Creator. It is when you recognize that your choice, as in this example, is not always the best one. And you surrender this choice to the Divine Creator that you are then, indeed, infused with the Divine Will, that you are guided and you are able to fulfill your contract. And so then are all things balanced. For this is the contract that each of you sign, or you agree to, before you come to Earth—is an attempt to balance at least part of that which you have foolishly sown in previous lifetimes.

It just so happens because this is the end of a cycle, many of you are being bombarded with many, many experiences, in which you have to make a choice, in order that this contract might be balanced for you to move into the next dimension of free choice and not by necessity."

—Hatonn

"They Meet Their Contract"

"There are ones that say they know nothing of the Light. They know nothing of what we speak. And yet, within their breast burns such a flame of Love for all of Earth Mankind that they can see nothing but the beauty, the perfectness in each of their brothers. They do not see race. They do not see color. They do not hear dialects. They do not question at strange language. But as their eyes gaze upon another, they are totally filled with *love* for that one. And yet, they profess to know nothing of *light!* And they would not say I would speak with them, for they have not time to hear my word. They are too busy helping others. And the veil has fallen for those ones just as the veil has fallen for you. And yet they meet their contract. And they are ones that shall carry Mother Earth thru this new day."

Received by Tuieta　　　　　　　　　**—Theoaphylos**

30

PHOTO BY KEVIN LAHEY

CHAPTER ONE

NETWORK OF LIGHT

SET OUT
TO BRING IN

THE

HARVEST

PHOTO BY MICHAEL RADFORD

"When They Put Their Parts Together On the Council Table"

"Beloved Ones: This day let it be recorded that which shall be given unto them which have a mind to receive it. While I say: There are ones which are not of a mind to accept these Mine Words, it is for the ones which will to know the Truth. While there are ones which have one part of the whole, others have another part—yet none shall deny that which is given unto the other, for the Great Plan shall be revealed only in part, until one is fully liberated from all bondage—then he shall see and know the fullness of the Plan.

Now I say unto thee: Deny not that which another hast been given, for therein is folly. It is said that: When they so love each other, that they put their parts together on the Council table, they shall come to see the whole of the Plan. Let them become wise! Let them so love each other that they put all their efforts into the gaining of Light. The Ones which are of the Great and Mighty Council shall then give unto them greater revelation; and they shall walk humbly and upright before the great Tribunal and they shall be as ones prepared to partake of such knowledge as is available thru the Council."

Recorded by Sister Thedra — **Sananda**

"I Do Send Ones About The Land To Collect Thee"

"I am thyne elder brother who does speak. I am known of many names. I am Esu within myne Father's House. I am Sananda to ye ones who do walk of the New Day. And to ye ones whose eye is cast behind I am known as Jesus. But, I say to each I am the Christos. I am the Christos. Know as ye receive of me so are ye guided by Divine Light. I have cum to claim thee O'Brethren, I have cum to claim you. And I do send ones about the land to collect thee, that none shall be lost.

Now ones shall say, 'He speaks not thru this one.' Or, 'He speaks not thru that one's pen.' So be it, if this is as they would think. But I say to them, the day shall fall upon their head when they shall recognize of these ones I have sent unto them. For I have sent ones across the land that each might hear of myne word, that each might receive. And these ones do cum as my priests, as myne priestesses. They do cum as myne handmaidens and myne manservants. And they do cum with myne authority. And that which I do put within their mouth. Receive ye and kno ye receive of myne word. Receive ye and kno they do speak with myne authority. Now it is I am thyne elder brother, I am the Christos.
Selah   Selah   Selah   Om ni di eno cum eta
Received by Tuieta

"We Work With All Of These Light Groups"

"I am Sananda. I have come to you this evening to express Myself to you to make known that I am desiring so much to bring together all those Groups of Light into the Glory of full fruition from the seed which I planted two thousand years ago as Jesus. Therefore, I desire so much that all Groups of Light become closer tied together, for We are one and therefore, We work with all of these Light Groups.

We ask that you all come to know yourselves as the Beings of Light which you are. Therefore, look no more toward the appearance World. Realize now that you are truly Beings of *Light;* that you are a part of that which We are. *United we stand!* That it is the Law, now united with the flesh. Even those who are the Leaders in the political arena shall follow the Law, (which you are in Action) and that Law will go forth. And that which has been prepared for eons and eons can be consummated and brought to fruition in the whole Solar System.

We are many Who are working with you in order to bring the Plan to consummation. Each one must know how important your part is so that you can fulfill it. You must act in confidence of that which you are and with the assurance of knowing that the place where you are is the 'Law in you in Action,' which opens the Way for Us, as you go forth taking your rightful place within the government of the I AM Nation, that is formulated of those who know their place in the Hierarchy." **—Sananda with Archangel Michael**
From: The Voice of Universarius

"A Network That Covers the Entire Globe"

"My Children of Light: The time of the Coming of the Lord is here. 'Let Light and Love and Power restore the Plan on Earth.' Picture a satellite high above the surface of the planet. Look down and see a vast interconnecting web of Light, a network that covers the entire Globe. This is the power of My Light Workers. It makes a glow that radiates out from the world of man.

Picture also a vast out-pouring of *love/power* from above to reinforce all those individual lights. This is My Love to you, each and every one. Each is interdependent upon the other. I need you, as you need Me. Together we shall make the Plan work out.

My Beloved, know that thy cry has been heard on high, that Peace, Justice, Harmony and Sharing must permeate the hearts of all before the Plan is to commence on a world-wide basis. This is where you come in. Radiate your Light and Love. It covers a vast sphere and encompasses those around you. It will have its effect."

I AM thy brother in the Light
I AM the Good Shepherd calling to My Lambs
I AM Christ Jesus
I AM Sananda

Channel: Bluebird   From: **The Voice of Universarius**

"The Quest To Go Beyond The Summit"

"If one has the strength and that which is called the quest to face that which is called a future sunrise, the quest to be beyond the summit, when you have the desire to do that you will always find *joy*, because in that there is no longer stagnation or looking back, and falling over yourselves. There is always something beyond the horizon that beckons and that of course is called 'future tense.'

There is Grand things in your days to come, all of which the least of are not boring. Many changes to be certain, but all for the ripening and the beauty of life. Life is the grand reality, it is the forever and ever and ever existence."

Channeled by J.Z. Knight   **—Ramtha**

"I Shall Speak of One Called Ramtha"

"Sori, Sori—I shall speak of one called Ramtha—yea I shall speak of him called Ramtha wherein he hast been called the Ram—which he is—for I know him for that which he is. When it is come that they know Him as I know Him, they shall cry out to him for mercy, for forgiveness for their foolishness for they know not that which he does—why he does that which is new unto them—for they are yet in darkness, clinging to their puny opinions, preconceived ideas, creeds and dogmas.

I say this One called Ramtha has many faces for His Wisdom is Complete. He has the Wisdom of the ages and he knows what he is about. He goes and comes thru many an age, he goes thru the galaxies as a free born Son of the Father Solen Aum Solen. No man is His judge, no man says nay to Him for he is above him who sets himself up. He has his hand within the Fathers—he sits not with the places of darkness wherein they speak to be heard of man. He comes with purpose and he is free from all forepreachments, presorcery. Ye shall find him a faithful Servant of the Light. So be it and Selah."
Recorded by Sister Thedra **—Sananda**

"He is Involved With the Entire Universe"

Question for Ashtar: 'What is your relationship to Jesus?' —Tuella.

"The same as yours. He is a revered and respected great Being of Light proceeding from the government of the Great Central Sun. He is a beloved Teacher through this entire universe, known and loved by all. His sacrifices for the cause of Light are tremendous above that of any other, and for this planet He has truly earned His position of World Teacher. However, He is involved with the entire universe and not simply this planet. His prestige is much more prodigious on other worlds than on this planet, where He has been scorned many times."
Received by Tuella **—Ashtar**

"A Link in the Great Chain of Ground Forces"

"The *network, consciously* accepted, becomes a great force for the ongoing of our program toward the rescue of, and assistance to, the planet. Even in New Age circles there must be a falling away of technical differences and an emphasis upon things on which there is agreement. Regardless of the partic-

ular slant or emphasis of truth, there must be a *conscious* desire to become a link in the great chain of ground forces rather than to stand alone. It is this *conscious* desire to be a *conscious operating* portion of the whole, that will create the proper atmosphere for the uplifting of frequencies I have described."
Received by Tuella **—I AM Andromeda Rex**

"The Children of Israel"

Question: "Could you tell us what it means when we are referred to as 'the children of Israel?' "

"At this time I shall not go into a great depth of detail, but I shall merely say that this is a designation of the children of God. 'Ye ones of Israel' is another way of saying to you ones of Earth that you are the children of God."
Received by Tuieta **—Monka**

"For All Are Children of God"

"Oh yes Earth man, soon you shall recognize that these areas that you call the great 'religions' of your world are in Truth but portions, are in truth but steps to be taken as you evolve toward that one which is known to you as God. Now someone on Earth would follow of this one, and some would follow of that one. And you ones are inclined to follow of the teachings of the one known to you as Jesus. And it is at this time that I speak of that which he added for all Earth man. For you see he did not come to be worshipped or adored. He did not come to be elevated in your eyes. But he came as the simple man, and he came as the simple teacher, that he could speak with each one face to face, that his eyes could see that he was that which he spoke. And so he brought this added dimension. And he said to you to love one another. And he said to love of that Divine essence that's within yourselves. And he spoke of helping one another. He demonstrated these things constantly as he was on your plane. For even as a small child, when I first met him, he demonstrated these things. Now what is this love? What is this that he spoke of?

To love one another is to recognize the divinity that is the Eternal spark of another's soul. To love is to let this Divine spark go forth along its chosen path, knowing that your paths cannot be the same. To love is to hold forth your hand to assist another with no thought of a return. To love, as this one my brother spoke, is to bask in all that is, is to see the Divine essence in all that is about, and all that is within. To love is to elevate no man above another, but to recognize the worth of each. This thought, o'ones of earthly plane, is one you have great difficulty with, for you tend to lean to elevate one above another, or to put down below another. This was not what this one brought to you. For all are children of God, and all children are equal within the eye of their parents."

Received by Tuieta   **—Djwal Kul**

"Each One has a Part"

"Beloved Ones—It is given unto Me to be One of the Host—And I Am Come that ye might be given the assistance necessary unto thine learning, as each one has a part and *no two parts are alike.* Yet All parts blend in One Harmonious Whole—where there is beauty and symmetry. I say there are no rough and ugly edges within the Whole—for All fragments and small parts shall fit together as One Beauteous Whole when the Plan is finished. There shall be light and dark—there shall be Golds and Blues of many hues, yet not One Piece shall be out of place—or in any way misplaced. These shall be as the 'Whole' and not one part or piece shall be discounted."

Recorded by Sister Thedra

"You Possess the Greatest Jewel in the World"

"You see you just don't know what you really are. You don't know how precious it *is* that you are. *You possess the greatest jewel* in the world, and you throw it away!!! You don't know what I see! And before leave I you again from this plane, I desire that at least you see it. And then if you want to spat upon it then So be it, that is the will of God. And yet if you embrace it you can *see* the *will of God.*

Love what you are—that way you can Love God. If you don't love yourself you can never fathom the beauty of God. Love yourself. You will never know how important you are until you do. And alas when you have embraced the value of beauty of self, of charity of self, of glory of self, God of self, you can embrace the whole of humanity without judgement, know you that? You can love them because you know that what they are doing they are wanting to do, without encumbering yourself to think you have to save them, no one ever will. It is up to personal self for salvation. It is God within salvation. Not dogmas, rituals. Charity begins within, Love begins within, Grace begins within, allowing begins within. Be all you can be, for all that you can be will Light the way for many others that want to see."

Channeled by J.Z. Knight   **—Ramtha**

"He is the Lord God of the Solar System"

"This day let it be established, that there are many spheres, many orbs, many planes, many places thruout the Solar System—Systems beyond thine System; Systems too numerous to count—each bearing life—life more glorious than thou has known upon thine orb of Earth. Yet Mine Beloved Ones: It is given unto Me to Know these of which I speak. I say, I know Systems without number, too numerous to count, and these are of the Father's creation. He hast given unto

42

PHOTO BY SISTER THEDRA

Mine keeping, the planet Venus, and for that matter I have adopted the little star called Earth—for wast it not said that I came unto Her when She was in dire distress? It is so—so shall I always hold Her dear unto Mine heart, and I shall not forsake Her now.

While it is given unto Me to be the Lord of Venus, I say unto thee: Mine Beloved Brother Sananda, hast chosen to come into this Solar System as the Lord God of this System. I tell thee: He is the Lord God of the Solar System, and He hast as yet not finished His Work therein, for He hast but a short while ere it is finished. Then He shall go on unto yet other world—other Systems which ye know not of. For this is He now preparing Himself; and there are Ones being groomed to take His office of Lord God, for He shall have yet another—another beyond His present station.

While I say, others are being groomed for His office—that which He now holds, I say: Thou too art being prepared for greater places, parts. Waste not thine energy, for it is now come when great things shall be demanded of thee, and ye shall be as ones called upon for that which shall be given unto thee to do—which shall be for the good of the Whole. While I say unto thee: Thou as yet knoweth not the great work which hast been accomplished while thou hast walked blindly, I say: Thou hast not been aware of the great things which hast been accomplished by thine work—thru thine efforts. So be ye as ones blest, and be ye alert, for I am come that it be so."
—I AM thine Older Brother and thine Sibor, **Sanat Kumara**
Recorded by Sister Thedra

♦**About This Photo:** "It is the manifestation of the Mother Eternal and it was by appointment that the manifestation was photographed."
Recorded by Sister Thedra   —**Sananda**

"A Fuller Revelation"
"The Spiritual Hierarchy of the Solar System has concluded that man has reached that point in his spiritual awakening when a fuller revelation of this closing portion of the Divine Plan for Earth may be revealed to him."
Received by Tuella   —**Lord Kuthumi**

"I Now Come as Yogunda"
Paramahansa Yogananda
"Bless you now, each and all of God's Children everywhere, as Hilarion has said and we always include everybody; for there is no one upon the Planet Earth who does not merit our Love and affection and even attention. Of course about 95% of them do not know that we are giving them any Love or attention and there is a large percentage that would even resent this attention and Love if they knew we were given it to them. Such a travesty upon human intelligence! But this is the way it is and we can change only a small fraction of it, but we try."
From the Voice of Universarius   —**Yogunda**

"New Wonders and Increased Happiness"
"Know that when you attune to the God within, that you will not be deceived. The time of decision is *now!* Your faith is soon to be rewarded with increased knowledge. The worlds which lie now within your grasp will be filled with new wonders and increased happiness.

We join forces at this time to welcome Earth's humanity into that new world. The choice is yours. Listen to your heart and know that the Light will prevail over darkness and ignorance of humanity's spiritual birthright."
Received by Carol Hall   —Conference transmission from
Korton, Hilarion, Ashtar & Aljanon

"Because They Share, They Send Forth Love, Wisdom and Purity"

"At this time, as you have been made aware by various others from higher dimensions, the energies to Earth are now being concentrated to Light workers and those that would truly and earnestly travel of their path. I will add here, that you might understand, we speak of you blessed ones as Light workers but know you there are Light workers that do not realize the higher dimensions at this time. These are our ones that are working not on the conscious level but inwards they are working on a conscious level, because they share, they send forth love, wisdom, truth and purity to all that touch their path. I would just caution you that because there are ones that do not believe in communication with the higher realms, such as we are experienceing right now, there are ones still that travel their path that are true. Do not become conceited, do not become content with your style for there are many paths, as there are many styles, to return to the Divine Creator.

Man of Earth has a tendency and I would say in this particular cycle more so than any other, to put down that which he does not understand or he does not accept as his own. This is the pity, this is the pity. Man's ears have shut off our voice that he has not the opportunity to hear us. He gathers of his wisdom by reading ancient books and by hearing the ancient teachings. For one that travels of his path in this way it is doubly hard for he is not aware of the day to day guidance, the day to day whisperings that are so close, that are available to him. For these ones I weep and I shall rejoice at the day that we can all sit together as one that they might hear first hand our words, our lessons, that they might truly feel our love that is shared with them. But these ones have chosen to come to Mother Earth at this time to enter at this particular cycle. This has been their choice. They have chosen also that they should travel of their path with a measure of blindness, that their eyes not have the opportunity to see, that their ears not have the opportunity to hear, that they might make their strides in a different manner than yours.

Dear ones, the final hours, the final hour is with you. The sorting has begun and indeed, each is being sorted according to their place. Now there shall be ones that shall read of my word and they shall say this causes fear within them. Not fear my friends, my brothers and sisters, not fear but may it cause joy and may it cause rejoicing. For as the sorting has begun, so soon shall you be lifted from this state, so soon shall the cleansing be that Mother Earth might don her new garment, that she might be made ready to receive the Sons, the Daughters of God. Yes, this is her role in the New Day for she has served most gallantly, she has served most patiently. And it is now that she prepares to rise up that she might be the pathway for the Sons, for the Daughters of God. I am Maitreya who does speak with you. Blessings to each. Feel of the Light. Know the Light is with you. Be the Light as you go forth. Be watchful, be joyful and know ye the hour is with thee."

Received by Tuieta   **—Maitreya**

"Few Which Dare to be Their Own Carter"

"And there are few which dare to be their own carter; and the carter is one which can say for himself that which way he shall go. And he shall find his own way; and therein is wisdom. For there are none so foolish as those who wait for the herd; therein is folly!"

Recorded by Sister Thedra   **—Sananda**

46

"You Will See God In Your Lifetime"

"With this that I speak to you of, the Christ, the God, the eminence of Holy and Divineness, can be understood by you—you will lift the entire frequency of the world! It will be lifted. For what you are *feeling, indeed!,* what you are *thinking,* what you are *experiencing* will ripple through the consciousness on all planes including this one.

You lift and feed your brothers by your thoughts and when the Christ is resurrected, that which is termed—the whole of the world will be shaken by the tremors of its effects, so it will be. You are the Light of the world. Love what you are, for you are loved. Regard yourself in high esteem, for you are esteemed! And know you have added to the quality of existence of all life, see and unseen, and for that you are purposefully needed. You didn't know that before, because who cared if you lived or died? Who cared if you wept or laughed? What difference in the state of affairs could you possibly have made? And by your meager existence who ever noticed? I *have noticed!* And I am here to tell you, you are needed and you are a treasure beyond treasure. That your life it is indeed important. For the times they are a changing and you my beloved entities, you will see God in your lifetime, you will see *the harrowing of ten thousand Armadas.* You will see Light that will fill the void. You will feel the thunder, you will feel the confusion, you will feel the peace. You my beloved entities will see *the new day* when all is wiped away, washed away, and made into a *new kingdom.''*
Channeled by J.Z. Knight   **—Ramtha**

"Ready and Willing to Assist"

Beloved Ones: There are mighty ones within the realms of light which are ready and willing to assist thee; for it is given unto them to be prepared for that which they are to do—for they have given of themself that ye might have thine freedom, even as they have theirs. I say unto thee, be ye as ones prepared to serve selflessly and knowingly. They walk not in darkness for they have been given their freedom from bondage. They weary not of waiting—they weary not of well doing, they are a patient lot. I say unto thee be ye likewise—for this do I say; weary not. I say unto thee; there are many which labor with thee in the hours of thine unknowing—and therein is wisdom for they know that which is necessary—and that which is for the good of all. I say they have the wisdom and the power and they have prepared themself for this day. I say unto thee these are thine Older Brothers, Thine Sibors (teachers) which labor long with thee without recognition or credit. I say they are a patient lot—for they ask nought for themself—they have everything at hand—for they have but to speak the word and it becomes manifest before them—while thine needs hast been supplied through and by their grace. I say unto thee, they give credit where credit is due, unto the Father from which comes their help. I say unto thee; give credit unto them for thine well being—unto the Father for thine being—and unto thineself for being the brothers which carry out the mandates given unto thee, this thine responsibility at this time. And as thou preparest thineself so shall ye receive. I say, *as Thou art prepared so shall ye receive—let it be as the Father wills—so be it.''*

—I AM thine Mother Eternal

CHAPTER TWO

HEAVENLY SIGNS - IN BRIGHT LIGHTS

ASHTAR COMMAND

PHOTO BY KEVIN LAHEY

"We Salute the Ashtar Command"

"I, Michael, do, without reservation, wholeheartedly endorse the work of Ashtar in the Name of the Brotherhood of Light. As Universal Statesman and Ambassador, his efforts have the fullest extent of my Authority behind them. Our governing Spiritual Hierarchy (see message entitled "Cosmic Hierarchy") has commissioned him to his task and sent him forth as an able representative of the policies and program set in order by that Hierarchy. I stand behind his efforts, his decisions and his works, to defend and protect, to educate and exhort the race of mankind to lift themselves higher in their aspirations and desires to walk the Christ Pathway as torches of Light.

We of the Governing Body of this Universe have found it necessary and proficient to enlist the services of these many highly endowed individuals who have chosen this service as a gesture of brotherhood, to assist your planet and thereby guide the destiny of the entire Solar System into a higher dimension of life.

The day will come when the men of Earth will rise up and call him blessed who has served as leader of this volunteer force, guided their coordination, broadcast their messages to Earth in a multitude of ways, to spread the good news of the Kingdom of God on Earth. We salute the Ashtar Command and all that it embodies, as well as all that it has accomplished and shall accomplish for the fulfillment of the Will of God. Receive ye this great Man, with our blessings and our benediction."
Received by Tuella　　**—I AM Michael,** of the Lord's Hosts

"Come! See!—For There Shall Be Plenty To See!

"Be ye as the Hand of Me and give unto them this Word, that it might be known unto them. For I declare unto them this day. A Power far greater than man hast known, shall be poured out upon the Earth, and man shall see the manifestation thereof. I say, they shall stand in awe of the Power which shall be made manifest before them.

Now it is come when the Heavens shall declare the Glory of the Heavens, and the 'pore' (bodily vehicle) shall be the 'pore', and the 'pore' shall have no power to close up the heavens, for it shall be opened up, and they shall have great fear, and they shall run and hide their face. There shall be ones which shall run forward and declare the Glory of the Heavens; they shall say: 'Come! See!'—for there shall be plenty to *see!*

I speak unto thee that they might be prepared—so let it be."
　　　　　　　　　　　　　—I AM come that it be,
Recorded by Sister Thedra　　　　　　**Sananda**

"There are Several Million"

"I say unto thee: There are several million which are within the place wherein I am—as ones prepared to enter into thine world as earthlings—as the ones of Earth—and They need not be born of woman—for they are Masters—Masters of the Elements—They Know the Law governing the Elements."
Recorded by Sister Thedra　　　　**—Sanat Kumara**

"We Come From Many Light Years Away"

"Greetings to you my friends this day, for we come to you my friends this day, for we come to you from vast distances in Space. We come to thee to share with you the blessings that we have to share with mankind, that ye, in turn will share with each other.

God bless you for opening your sanctuary and inviting us to partake within your Service, to be one with thee, and to show your love and openness to us from the outerspace—for we are oft times rejected by mankind.

God bless you, for we know that we do have a place where we can come to and we can inform you of the happenings in time as they pass by. God bless you for sharing your love and being with us here and to allow us to be with you—not in fear, but in love.

God bless you, for we come from many light years away. We have been patrolling your area and your skies for great periods of time. We have been the protectors, and we have been the ones who have inhabited your Earth plane and are responsible for the great scientific advances that have taken place. For we come as one, as you, and we share the knowledge of the past with you, for the future—for it is by this means that your world shall go ahead."
Recorded by Cornelius, Edmonton, Alberta, Canada

"There Will Be Signs In The Heavens"

"The Ashtar Command is present overhead everywhere upon the planet. There are thousands and thousands of ships in our many fleets that make up the Ashtar Command. We are the Etherians, and ours is the authority that controls the entire Space Program for the planet.

In the coming decade there will be signs in the heavens that your glib talking officials will be unable to deny. For an awakening has come at last to the population of the planet and an awareness of the purpose of help of a high order coming to mankind, ever closer, every day that passes.

In the Name of the salvation of the life of Humanity, we ask that you would receive our words and *welcome us to speak in your assemblies!*

If the space is made, the spokesman will appear!

This message is sent to planet Earth by the members of the Ashtar Command.

Peace On Earth! Goodwill Toward Men!"

Received by Tuella

"What Will Happen To Them"

"The questions have been voiced, and we have felt these questions concerning ones that are not involved in Light groups, as to what will happen to them. It has been stated before, and I shall emphaticaly state it once more, that all of those on Earth that believe in the Divine Force, the Divine Creator, the Father—Mother God, the Omnipotent One, all of these; all of your ones that do believe; that have love in their hearts for others; that seek not to intentionally or willfully harm others, so shall you come forth, so shall each one come forth. At this time, we have the opportunity of speaking with various Light ones, in the attempt, that we might reach more of you on Earth. This is not to say that you are the only ones that shall be involved, for all ones of Truth, all ones of Love, all ones of Light shall be delivered. Do not be concerned of this."
Received by Tuieta   **—Ashtar**

"Their Lights Will Soon Be Seen In Your Heavens Again"

"And the third is called interdimensional, there are kingdoms above Terra that you have never seen, there are dimensions above Terra that you do not know of. There is Terras that exist as Terras but in another thought another

56

understanding, and this thought and understanding also has understandings upon it such as you.

We have Higher brothers that are in a different time, a different dimension. And they too have the accessiblity of their primitiveness that is termed aeroships, and can materialize themselves through dimensions in time. And theirs, master, indeed and their light to which they use is white and it is but a moment of their use.

Whosoever goes into the wilderness and looks into the heavens and sees a brilliant whiteness, you'll see the Divine ships that are called aeroships. Ones as it were indeed, that do not intimidate these peoples but love them. They have a kinmanship for they are of a greater light and a greater understanding than that even of our brothers that live within the center of this plane Terra. Though they be higher in thought and more refined, the Great Light Master, indeed, knows it's purity only and nothing else. Their Lights will soon be seen in your heavens again. They are the Novas, they are the Stars, it was they that presented that which is termed the Star of Bethlehem, it was a great ship and nothing else.''

—Ramtha

Question: ''I know that you had said that the Star of Bethlehem was in fact a space ship?''

''It is called a Mothership.''
Channeled by J.Z. Knight   **—Ramtha**

'' 'Astara'—Reflecting Forth Specific Light Patterns''

Question: ''Could you please give us the meaning of this eight-pointed star that is being seen in the North?''

''I am Monka to reply. Thank you for allowing me the opportunity to come forth. My Blessings to each of you. You have been told in your Holy Writ, as well as through seers, through those that receive the Word, the guidance in various ways that each will be given a sign, will see a sign, will recognize a purpose and a direction. This what you report seeing is being seen, not only by you but by other ones, throughout your northern hemisphere. This is not a star as you would consider a star being a body of formed matter, such as your Earth or your moon or the planets. But this star is Astara. This is one of our ships that is reflecting forth specific light patterns that might be picked up by various ones on Earth. To you it would seem as a star. Indeed it is one of our larger ships that is in a stationary position at this time. As you gaze at this and your thoughts send forth love and harmony, and you reach out to combine energies with those that are in the ship so shall you receive a reply to your thoughts. I trust this answers your question.''
Received by Tuieta   **—Monka**

''Bewildered by What You See''

''Yes, dear friends, the *craft* Do exist, and there are also those who 'man' them, who are coming within the frequencies which make them visible . . . to the ordinary people, including those in responsible positions, and those in the Defence Departments of your countries who would deny our actuality.

Because you are naturally curious about Nature in all its manifestations we feel it is time that we turned another page in the Book of Life, so that we may help you to expand your vision. To us, you are 'newly awakened'—having been asleep for many centuries of your Time-Cycle; you are 'rubbing your eyes' now, and are bewildered by what you see.''
From: Axminster Light Center, England   **—Captain Zoa**

"Through The Etheric Window"

Question: "Could you Please tell us more of the etheric window?"

"I am Hatonn to reply. This is an area, or indeed I should say, there are specific areas about your planet that are freer from the contamination of Earth than others. These are areas that are in direct relation to specific land marks upon your Earth. To pass through these areas is to travel from one dimension to another. As we enter your ethers through the window we have the opportunity to change our vibrational pattern that we might be observed by ones of Earth. Or we also have the opportunity to maintain our present vibrational rate that we are unobserved by you. But in the event we would want ones of Earth to observe us, or to observe one of our ships we would enter through the etheric window, and lower our vibrational rate that the molecular structure would be condensed thus forming the image for the outurned eye. When this happens one of our ships then is locked into this vibrational frequency, until such time as they can again escape through the etheric window out into the pure ethers farther away from Earth.

The etheric windows about Earth move according to the energy patterns that are set up within the ethers around your planet. In these areas are the etheric windows that we might enter and we might leave at will. These are continually shifting about your planet though there are certain areas that are relatively stable. Here I would speak of areas over your mountain ranges called the Himalayas. There is also another window that is relatively stable over your area that is called the Bermuda Triangle. There is also another window that is close to your mountain called Mt. Shasta. There is also another window that is close to your lake in South America that is known as Titicaca. There are other windows about your Earth that are over your Polar Areas and over some of your various mountain ranges and areas over your Earth. I hope this has helped to answer your question."

Received by Tuieta **—Hatonn**

"When These Break Through The Veils"

"We have *craft-action* at all *density-levels*, and there are times when these break through the *veils*. When this happens, earth-man experiences visionary spectacles which are to him awesome in aspect. Those that emerge from the lower densities, create wild speculation, as their *forms* present a distortion to embodied third-density-senses.

Manifestations from the *higher-densities* are spectacular and command the *awe* of those who are not familiar with *light bodies,* and energy-fields by the *space fleet.*"

By direct dictation, thru Teska **—I AM . . . Krona**

"A Shuttle Ship That Was Observed"

"At this time, with your permission, I shall answer a question that was put forth earlier, and this was one concerning a publication of a shuttle ship that was observed beneath the waters off of your coast. Yes, this was one of our shuttle ships that was observed beneath the surface. And this one was left within this particular place until such time as a window opened within your ethers, that it could be removed with a minimal of energy output."

Received by Tuieta **—Hatonn**

"The Energy Windows"

"I have just completed exercises where we have watched for the windows, the energy windows, where we might enter into Earth's atmosphere. And then we would change our vibratory rate that we might again go through the window into our present dimension, your next one."

Received by Tuieta **—'D'**

PHOTO BY MICHAEL RADFORD

"When They Dip Into The Third Dimension"

"Aboard my command ship are many scientific instruments which gauge the intensity of the buildup of force within the fault lines and the strains that are being put upon the tectonic plates. These energies are measured very accurately without our having to come into visible formation in the third dimension. Here on our scanner, we have a cross-section of the fault lines as they pass through your own State of California. Enlarging the picture we can see the whole West Coast at a glance. Computers are no new play toys for earthlines, but have been used successfully to do our bidding through out "time." Our Computers tell of the heat buildup, which areas will most likely give problems next, and with this information we can then plot our strategy. The patrols are on a 24-hour surveillance mission and report back to the command with their findings. People of Earth are only aware of these craft, when they dip into the third dimension weaving energy lines (or threads). Energy is not just a dimensional phenomena but interpenetrates all dimensions and interacts with the characteristics of that dimension through which it flows. We can work with these lines of energy."

Received by Lucy Colson **—Marius**

"A Portion of Quiet Time"

"I would urge you to continue to look to the skies, to watch the stars that you might catch a glimpse of us. In your lifestyles of this day I would urge you as never before that you set aside a portion of quiet time that we might communicate with you. It is vital for your balance that this be done. We continue our activities here in preparation for your arrival."

Received by Tuieta **—I AM Monka**

"Our Computers are Activated by Thought"

"Let's just speak for a moment about computers. Oh, allow me to introduce myself, I am Hatonn. These machines that you have on Earth do serve of their purpose, but in the days to come you shall realize exactly how archaic they are. We have computers on our ships. And so do not doubt our reality, for I assure you, we are quite real. And we do have computers on our ships. But our computers are activated by thought. For instance, if we wish to tune into your circle we have but to look at the monitor, to concentrate our thoughts on this particular circle of Light and you immediately appear. I can see each of you right now quite clearly. And our pictures on our monitors, when we look at you ones of Earth, are not ones of dots and dashes and various matrixces. But we have a true picture of you. We can see the blush in your cheek. We can see the twinkle in your eye. And we can see the Light of your Soul, for your aura comes through quite clearly on our screens.

Should we wish to see the aura of a particular group all we have to do is concentrate our energies, our thoughts on this, and this is what appears on our screen, a rainbow of the auras that mingle, that become the aura of one group. For instance, if I concentrate on the aura of this circle I shall see predominately a golden-white Light. And there is a thin band of green, of lapis blue, and of indigo. But the predominant color of this group this night is a golden-white Light. So I know when I see this what energies you are receiving, what you are transmitting, and the at-one-ment of those of you that sit together. There is no disharmony in this group this night,

---

Note: Until the preceeding photograph was developed the ship was not seen. The photographer intended to capture the large orange cloud, of which you can see a small portion as this is an enlargement of the ship.

61

there is no discord. And it is evidenced by your aura. But now, how did I get started on auras when I was speaking of computers? Well, this lesson you needed to know anyhow.

But as I was saying, our computers are activated by thought. As you grow in your awareness, and you learn to control, to use your thoughts in truly the manner that they were intended, you shall be able to do many things that this day seem far beyond your grasp. Everything aboard our ships is computerized to be used by our thoughts. So you see, we have to arrive at a certain level, though that is not a good word, a certain attunement. For it would be possible for those that are out of tune to misuse this gift, which has been given to us. So just as we have the gift we also have the responsiblity that goes with it."

Received by Tuieta — **Hatonn**

"To Enjoy Intergalactic Unity and Cooperation"

"We are the Masters of the Korendor Hierarchy returning to you by permission of your group of Masters. We come to bring to your attention the nature of the relationship between the Galaxies and the various systems that make up this Universe. The Korendian group of planets and bodies that make up our Galaxy is in full cooperation with the Galaxy which supports your own solar system. Your world is striving to achieve the concept of One World—United in mission toward its people—while the Galaxies individually strive to press into action their people. Likewise, throughout the Universal realms there is a thrust from the great central governments to enjoy intergalactic unity and cooperation that will enhance life through the Universe as a Whole. This requires Love, cooperation and understanding on all dimensions and within all Universal dominions."

Received by Tuella — **We are the Masters of Korendor**

"Without Understanding There Is No Communication"

"Beloved Ones: With these Words I shall bless thee, for they are so designed that ye be blest. When there is communication one with the other, there is understanding; and without understanding there is no communication. And there is no communication. And there is no communication when one cuts himself off, one from the other; for this is it said: Be ye as "One"—let there be understanding, and communication.

While I say: Words are the lesser part of communication, and therein is the pity of it, for there is too much reliance put upon the spoken word, which but gives the smallest significance, unto the Truth—for the Reality is never conveyed by words, or language, such as thou art accustomed to. While the greater revelation is conveyed by way of Light Sources, which they know so little of, and which shall be as the future means of communication. These Light Rays shall carry great power, great weight, and nothing shall bar or distort these Rays, for they shall be directed unto the ones prepared to receive, and at no time shall they be intercepted by the enemy, which would destroy and distort, and use them to their own end, or nefarious schemes. I say: They shall not pilfer such power, neither shall they distort the Light for their own end.

So let it be said that we are Masters of such Light Rays/Beams, and We know the law governing such as ⚡ and therein is another story—be ye as ones prepared to receive it, for it shall be given unto thee."

—I AM thy Sibor and thy Older Brother, BEREAN
Recorded by Sister Thedra

"The Mother Ships are in their Designated Areas"

"But as I have said the countdown has come. We have started on our final. The sector commanders, the mother ships in their designated areas, at frequencies attuned to our beloved Commander-in-Chief and his word. As the word goes out, your skies shall be filled with hundreds of thousands of ships to assist, to lift, and to bring ones of Earth help during this period. There is time, my dear ones, but it is at a minimal. There is time. I would urge each of you to be strong in these the final hours. As you look about you, take notice of the signs and what is happening.

—**I AM Monka,** a most humble servant of the Radiant One. I am your friend, I am your brother of the galaxy. Good night."

Received by Tuieta

"He Shall Be As A Trail Blazer"

"The day arrives swiftly when one shall stand free from all gravitation of Earth, and he shall be as one free from the attraction of the Moon—he shall be as one free! I say, as one free, for the law of gravity shall not bind him unto the Earth. He shall go and come freely, and stand as one free. He shall be as one which has the crown of the Sun upon his head; he shall move freely thru the atmosphere, and he shall be as a trail blazer—he shall be as the forerunner of that which is to be done, that which shall be done."

Recorded by Sister Thedra   —**Sananda**

"Thousands of Shining Souls"

"We of the Universal Confederation, Guardians of your planet, are the reaping angels who shall come to separate the chaff and to gather the wheat into the Father's storehouse. We of other worlds have accepted this responsibility to your planet and your people. Our service to the Radiant One has been long and steadfast and loyal. In my assignment as coordinator of this program, it has been my privilege to personally meet and become acquainted with untold thousands of shining souls, who have come to offer their help in this service to humanity in its difficult transition. These are souls with a dedication to the Heavenly Father, and an awareness of themselves as Light beings of His Creation.

Many constellations, many galaxies, and even many other universes, are represented in this group that passes before me. This alliance has strengthened and contributed to the bond of love between all of our worlds, as our hearts have united in this program of evolution for Earth and its people.

You are now well on the way and off to a good start. Light is expanding upon you and within you. The hold of the dark ones is loosening each day that passes, and the stars in their courses are leading you on to your fulfillment. Trust us, for we are your friends. We come in Love and dedication to this great cause which will unite all worlds in peace and brotherly love. We are standing by, organized, alerted and ready in the twinkling of an eye to serve you as brothers.

Yield yourselves as instruments of Light upon your plant and channels of peace. Let Love control your Being and Love penetrate all of your affairs. Only those who live in Love for their fellow man are numbered for fellowhsip with us. Recognize and realize the Presence of the Beloved Christ in every other human face, and honor that Christ within. When you think upon us, remember that each of us who patrol your skies, is a manifestation of the Creator, even as you.

63

Do not let thoughts of approaching events overwhelm you. Instead, find your confidence and strength in the secret place of the Most High. Be still and know that the Father will never forsake you, when you put your trust in Him. We come to you as Brothers, in His Name. I am a Brother from other worlds."

Received by Tuella   **—I AM Matton**

cycle. There is one that is in between which takes you from a specific point in your evolution up to your present one, which is equivalent of your earthly 500 thousand years. For your information again and increased enlightenment, you are also ending that 100 year time in which you of Earth note specific changes.

There are four cycles that I have spoken of and indeed there are many more, but the first three are the major cycles that we are speaking of at this time. I trust this has answered your question."

Received by Tuieta   **—Hatonn**

"A Chronological Group of Events"

Question: "We have been told that there are three major cycles coming to an end at the same time. Could you please share with us additional information about this?"

"I am Hatonn to reply. And because of the current station that I hold as the statistician and record keeper for this portion of the universe, I shall be happy to share with you that limited knowledge which I have. Your first major cycle is that period from the last time that the Earth was cleansed up until its next cleansing. It is that period of time in which your continents, your oceans, your lakes, your rivers, etc., your topographical map is essentially that one that you know this day. This is one time of one particular cycle. And I specifically do not use years, for rather, the cycles cover a chronological group of events.

Your next cycle is that one that was ushered in when the Lord Sananda came to Earth as Jesus. That is your shorter

"I AM of the Brotherhood"

Question: "Monka, are you an ascended Master?"

"I am Monka to reply. And I must say my beloved one, I feel most humbled that you would consider such a question of me. I have travelled of my path just as you are travelling yours. No, I am not what you would call an ascended Master, though I assure you we work most closely with the one known to you as Jesus Sananda. However on my planet, I have been elected to varying positions of responsibility that others have felt that I might be capable to assume these duties.

Perhaps, your sense of closeness to me might be the result of the amount of energy that I have expended with those of you on Earth. In many instances for many of the Tribunals I sit as the representative for Earth to argue on behalf of you ones of Earth that you might be given opportunity. I sit as the

PHOTO BY MICHAEL RADFORD

PHOTO BY KEVIN LAHEY

representative on Tribunals to speak on behalf of Earth. So you see my dear one, no, I am not what you would consider an ascended Master, but I am of the Brotherhood, and I do serve with total commitment to the Light. And I am at the service and the disposal of our Beloved Sananda. I too am a brother who strives to grow along his path that I might evolve into a greater dimension, that I might be of greater service to all of universal mankind.''

Received by Tuieta   **—Monka**

"I Love You All Very Much"

"Hello, hello, hello, it is Aleva again to return and I am so happy to be back. And it seems like I have been gone from you so long. And I promise that I shall not stay that long again. Greetings beloved ones.

As I observe your circle I notice that we have some new energies coming forth, and I bid each of you a welcome. And know that you too share in my love even though that you are not aware of it, and you do not know me at this time. My name is Aleva, and I have just recently returned from my leave that I might return home to visit for a short period, before returning to my duties here on the command ship "Constellation." As you note, you ones, my assignment has been changed. And I am most joyful to be. Though, I will say at this hour our beloved Commander-in-Chief is not here on the ship with us. But I am told he shall return shortly. It is so beautiful here and it was so lovely to go home.

You see our home is somewhat different than it would be living in a ship, for I am from an area that is much more pastoral, and I am used to the hills and the gentle animals and all of that, which you do not have on your ships. For they are more efficient and more organized than they would be if there were rolling hills everywhere. But then you see not everyone would like rolling hills now would they? I am so pleased to return with you dear ones. And I am so pleased to feel the love that you so abundantly share with me, and know that I return it to you ten-hundred times that you might be bathed in the Light, in the love too.

Blessings to each of you. I have nothing specific to report at this hour, but I just wanted to pop in to say hello, hello, and that I love you all very much. Good night.''

Received by Tuieta   **—Aleva**

"Trips to Other Galaxies, To Meet the Beautiful Souls of Light"

"Greetings Earthean Brothers and Sisters: It was with great joy that Brother Korton told me, I Surnia was to begin my schedule for bringing forth "thoughts" of our activities on behalf of you on planet Earth. May I say to you that I, and many other women have had extensive training from my father, who is Kadar Monka, and many other teachers. We operate our Craft and fill in when the need arises. So you see we are, after many cycles, prepared to step in and fill the place of the male who has been assigned to duty at great distances. We also have received all the instruction to replace anyone of those duties when occasion demands "instant action" and the others are out away from home base.

I have worked and been taught many things by one whom I love very much called Soltec. *We* have taken many trips to other Galaxies, to meet the beautiful souls of Light, on survey missions, and also on what Soltec had as an assignment. He is an astro-physicist and has great knowledge concerning the travels through Space, and the debris encountered, and he has played a great role in making it safer for all of us here who are working under your Brother Jesus. It is such a pleasure to have *Him* as our Mentor, associate and comrade. He never appears as superior or boss (your earthean terms). The Light that surrounds *Him* whenever *He* appears is fabulous to behold, it extends way beyond *His* personage. The Planet of Alpha Centauri also we spend much time on, whenever we are not on duty, for it is the planet Soltec calls home. Soltec has great knowledge and study of Gasses, Masses of various substances, encountered in travel at such tremendous speeds of Light. We, each of us who are working in the Cosmic Event of Planetary change have learned to cope with all the conditions that would be encountered in travel whether local or Interplanetary. We, of course have learned the use of diplomacy, and although we are always treated as equals, we look up to instruction from those who have spent many more Cycles learning through actual experiences."

Channeled by KaRene   **—Surnia of Mars and K.O.R.**

"Trust is Imperative"

"Of course, if Earth's entities were to increase their awareness and realize that love is the only cure for what is plaguing the planet, the situation would quickly reverse itself. You who have this awareness can lessen the severity of the situation by projecting all the love that is within you to all you come in contact with, especially to adversaries and enemies, and, of course, to the planet itself. Become an example of love so others may see the proper way to live life. Every chance you get, help others to understand that love is the only real cure for the planet's problems. Use the Light as a shield against low vibrations so that you do not fall into the descending cycle.

Much help is available to you, so don't try to tackle this giant alone. And to repeat the message again—*trust* is imperative and will become more and more critical as the external illusion of chaos worsens. Be open to our help and as you have received it—so give it, but only if it is desired—never force it on another."

Channeled by the Light Group 'Universalia'   **—Christmon**

"Accept This In Faith"

"Greetings o'children of Light. I am Beatrix returned to speak most briefly with you if it is your pleasure.

We have asked of you in past days to concentrate your efforts, your energies, your thoughts on specific areas of your planet that those areas might be enfolded, encircled in the Love and the Light of the Magnificent One. At this hour, with the greatest of solemnity, I again ask that you hold your planet, your total planet in Light. No, I shall not discuss reasons. I would ask that you accept this in faith, and you would accept this with the same thoughtfulness that it is given to you. And now I shall take my leave of you for there are duties that call me to distant parts of your land. Good night my brothers and sisters.

Received by Tuieta   **—Beatrix**

Note: *Peace the 21st* is a movement of energies combined and concentrated towards such as the above each Solstice and Equinox. All who will, come together in groups or by themselves, to meditate and send Love to the planet, at 7:30 pm, on Sept. 21, Dec. 21, March 21, and June 21; in every time zone worldwide. All Light Groups and individual thoughts are powerful when sent forth as *one>< won.*

70

"An Unending Circle of Light and Love"

Question: "What is the best way for us to send Light and Love?"

"I am Monka to reply. Thank you dear sister, for your question for it is a most appropriate one. As we ask of you to share Light and to share love with others or with other parts of your Earth, I might give you this visualization for your consideration. Picture, if you will, that area or that individual which is the object of your attention, of your love. See them enfolded in the golden bubble of love, that they are centered within this. See the energy, the love, the Light that comes to you. See this come into your being, and see this go forth from your being to this one or to this place. And as you visualize these blessings coming into your being and going through your being, also visualize these blessings coming straight from the Divine Creator to this one, that you have an unending circle of Light and Love that is never ceasing and unbroken. Perhaps this example shall assist you as you hold others in Light and Love."

Received by Tuieta   —**Monka**

"They Know That the Essential Connection Is Love"

"In truth, there are more starfleets within Universe 45 of the Ashtar Command than ever before. We are in what you would think of as a 'holding pattern,' not only around planet Earth, but in your sun system and Universes 45, 46, and 47 as well. Vibrations of high magnitude are accelerating which could produce extremely (according to your Earth perceptions) negative manifestations upon planet Earth, and the sun system in which she orbits. So we are on hold, preparing to intensify our efforts if the Order is rendered to us.

The Eagelian Triad has concluded that it is no longer necessary to prove our existence by allowing our ships to be seen in great numbers. Too many Earthlings think of us as phenomena. We are no more phenomenal than you are. Too many Earthlings are only interested in the construction of our ships and what we look like in comparison to what you call 'human' or 'humanoid.' Those who are connected to our Essence and are united mind-to-mind are our true space brothers and sisters. There is too much work to do to spend our energy exhibiting our physical molecular forms to satisfy those whose only interest is in 'phenomenon of UFO sighting.' We have no need to prove our existence in physical form anymore than 'God' needs to prove His existence. Believe me, if we did not exist, you would not have the wonderful world of what you call 'science fiction,' nor would you have ever built a rocket powerful enough to land a human upon your own orbiting satellite. And if the Creator did not exist, we would not be and you would not be.

What we are doing is establishing starbases all over Universe 45 and preparing vibratory shields for innocent planetary bodies in your sun systems and surrounding sun systems. What we are doing is taking many of those of high consciousness aboard during their Earth sleep state and preparing them and teaching them those things they must know in order to assist us in the event that some of your entities begin playing with your nuclear toys. And what your guides and master guides are trying to do is create a Universal Love Consciousness. You need to start listening.

You must also become more attuned to the fact that Earth has entered the New Age and her vibratory rate is increasing and intensifying as well. Earth is becoming less dense in her own preparation to release her outer crust in order to give birth to the New World. Those of high conscious awareness are likewise becoming less dense. As you become less dense yourself, you will become unaware of denser forms than yourself.

For those of you who need to see our molecular forms in order to believe, we are sad. For those who can raise their vibratory rates to experience us in a higher dimension, we are pleased. But, for those who are open enough to allow a connection with us mind-to-mind and understand our united essence, these are our true star brothers and sisters, for they know that the essential connection is love."

—Apollo, Atlantan Starfleet Commander,
from the Starship 'Golden Crysolis'
Channeled by those of the Light Center 'Universalia'

"On the Greatest Level of all 'He' is that which Holds You Together"

"God is, one level of gross matter without counting number, all things. On another level He *IS* the time flow of the difference of dimensions, the warp, indeed a parallel universe. On another level indeed He *IS* the spectrum called *light* that give the supportiveness to matter and indeed on the Greatest Level of all *He Is* that which holds you together, indeed! Know you that which is termed your scientists term the little substances that holds your cells together? They have referred to it, as it were, quite dramatically indeed, as cosmic glue. How else and how much better to explain what it *is* that holds you together."
Channeled by J.Z. Knight   **—Ramtha**

"Such Joy, Such Love and Enthusiasm"

"Hello! Hello! Hello! I am Aleva to return. And oh, I have so much to tell you. And I have so much joy that I want to share with you. And isn't everything just beautiful. I must tell you, I finally have been initiated. Yes, I have been initiated, really and truly, honestly initiated! For I went before the Council! And if I had been one of Earth, it would have been just like I had received my 'wings' or something. Before—because—Oh, dear, am I going too fast for you? Well, there were those of us that were taken before the Saturnian Council and we received our initiation. And oh dear ones, I just couldn't wait to return to share it with you for it was most beautiful. And our Beloved Lord Sananda came and he touched me. And he blessed me. And he said what I was doing was important. And I knew it was important but for our Lord, our Commander-in-Chief to really tell me this, it was just tremendous. And I was so excited. And I just had to share this with all of you.

There is so much going on. And there are many ones of us that are being reassigned to various ships and to various places as we get ready for the next stage that's going on. And its just a most busy time for all of us. And those of us that were initiated and received our promotions, it is just the greatest thing. For I have been changed to a different ship now. And I will be on the same ship as our Lord Sananda is on. And it will be so beautiful to be able to meet each one of you there as you come aboard! There! I do hope I haven't gone too fast. And I do hope you've been able to understand. Dear ones, I just want to share with you, for you see you have been my first eartheans that I have communicated with, and I feel most close to you. And I want you to know that I shall be there to greet each of you as you join with us.

There has been some rearrangement, some reassignments here on the ships. And various ones have assumed additional

72

PHOTO BY KEVIN LAHEY

PHOTO BY ZENON MICHALAK

responsibilities. And though I still am the official greeter for the ship, I shall be working more in a teaching capacity, both for the ones that come from Earth and for those from the other planets and places. For you see I have finished, or rather I should say, I have completed, my tour of various planets and stars within this universe where many of you will be going in the distant day, after you have had your sojourn on the ship. And I shall be giving you brief instructions along this line. My goodness! In your earthean terms it will be that I will be a 'tour guide,' for I shall be preparing you to go to your next areas of assignments. But I have gathered to myself those bits of information that I feel will be beneficial to you when you arrive here, to help you to understand what is going on here in this vessel, as well as on the various places where you will be going.

Now I shall be silent and let our dear beloved Commander Monka speak with you for I have 'stepped in' even though I did this with his permission. I shall await him. Thank you beloveds and blessings be to each of you. For my heart is warmed when I can come forth and speak with you. And I feel your love as it comes forth. And I send it back to each of you ten, times ten, times ten for I love you each. Good night.''
Received by Tuieta **—Aleva**

Monka: ''I am Kadar Monka returned. And I shall speak most slowly to allow 'this one' (Tuieta) an opportunity to catch her breath that we might continue at a more comfortable pace—I would say one that is mutually comfortable. Our small one has such joy, such love and enthusiasm. I must say she is quite contagious. But in earthean terms if you would be to contact a contagious disease, would not this one she transmits be a delightful one to have?''

"Some of the Light Displays That Have Been Observed"

''And now it is my pleasure and happiness to share with you a dear friend from the distant plant of Litikus. Captain Arma has been with the fleet for a long period of time. His particular assignment has been a group of ships that patrol your northern hemisphere, particularly the northern sections of your United States and of Canada, I would say to you from the middle of your United States up to that point which you know as the North Pole. Some of the light displays that have been observed on Earth, and have been credited to the aurora borealis, have in fact been activities of Captain Arma and his squadron. And though many of you have travelled great distances in your sleep state you have not travelled to this distance. And so I shall be silent for a most brief moment that your dear Captain might speak with you, and share some of his thoughts and his observations.''
—Monka

Captain Arma: ''Good evening, good evening, good evening. Salutations from all of us in Squadron CEE. We have patrolled your skies for a period of time you of Earth would call a number of years. We are quite familiar with each of you, your energy patterns, and indeed, the energy patterns of all Light Groups within this northern sector.

Our ships are all ships that are manned ships, so there are many ones of us that follow closely your activities and your progress. My message shall be most brief for I am not one that is familiar with communication with you ones of Earth. But I would offer to you at this hour our love and our thoughts to help you to travel your path, to help you prepare for your days ahead, and to let you to rejoice in this moment. On behalf of Squadron CEE, may I say good night and may peace abide within each of your hearts.''
Received by Tuieta **—Captain Arma**

"We Hope To Make Inroads For the Inflow of Light"

"We who are of the Andromedan council are in the Earth's atmosphere at this time for the express purpose of contacts with our own. We have come as emissaries to the people of Earth to assist them in finding the solution to their problems. Chiefly We are arbitrators and will mediate any disputes that can be settled through Our guidance. We come to offer a solution to the problem of hatred, brother against brother. The weapons must be cast aside, for when one is faced with the cold unfeeling metal of destruction, one cannot open his heart to the antagonist. We hope to bring enlightenment to those who are weary of war, to give solace to the grieving women who have lost loved ones: Husbands, fathers, children. The time has come for this to cease, but it will be a long drawn out process before We get an ear that will listen to what We have to say.

The Shining One will return to walk the planet among His own. But at this time the streets are not safe for Him, though harm Him they could not. But His Presence will evoke such energies as will be uncontrollable by many, at both ends of the scale, for good as well as evil. Thus you see the importance of Our mission. We need every Light Worker to join in a united meditative effort to ease the tension and evoke a climate of hope among the nations which are in turmoil and on the verge of chaos.

We must create an air of responsiveness that the Love energies will produce Light. This We are asking Earth's Light Workers to implement that Our efforts will not be in vain. During the Year as you know it, changes in planetary positions in the heavenly spheres are producing extremely high energy vibrations.

This must be utilized by those with the knowledge of such techniques for the good of the entire globe. By channeling Light into the troubled spots, by evoking the Angelic Hosts for assistance in opening the hearts of the antagonists to the Light, We hope to make inroads for the inflow of Light. Only when Light can penetrate those hearts will there be hope for a solution to be found.

We will call upon all Our resources, those from Our system so far across the galaxies, for this combined effort on behalf of Our little brothers of Earth. Those from Andromeda will be known to each other and will find a mutual link, similarities in many facets of their lives and dim remembrances, We will inform you of these when the time is deemed right and according to necessity. Many others are working in specific areas of the planet. Our particular sector is the Middle East.

The problems there only seem insurmountable when you put them in a time frame. We see the solution is far ahead but it is not an impossible goal. Time is being stressed now for the action to commence, for it to take seed and begin to root. We are inspiring Our compatriots to use their mental processes to fill the mental plane with proper thought forms to aid in this seeding process. Also, the Transmutation of the astral plane to clear the emotional forms so distorted through the ages is a necessity before the fertilization of the mental plane can be effective. It is a preparation of the soil before the planting. All must proceed in proper sequence.

Therefore We are enlisting those who will be concerned with Our project. This is a call to those willing to lend their thought power to the solution of this tremendous problem. It can be done but this preparatory work which is less 'glamourous,' less appealing to many who want to take physical action. But as you well know, things, events and activities are first formulated on the mental plane before manifestation on the physical. Therefore the necessary work must be done simultaneously on the mental with the clearing of the debris from the astral in order to clear the way for the appearance on the physical.

To this end We will be seeking out assistance, and to those who know their roots are in the Stars, We are sure of response. The time is coming when these thoughts will be seen by those with the inner vision. Then indeed will be the work in unison, for they will be building with a more definite attitude towards the purpose. The hardest part and the most tedious is the preliminary stages in which We are now involved, and in which little fruit is seen from the labor extended. Those who respond now, may see this take root and come to fruition. They may well see the flowering though it takes ages. The rapidity of the results will be dependent on the number working steadfastly toward the solution of the world problem. Many hands and minds joined in such a project will Lighten the burden for the Whole of humanity.

Brothers and sisters, do not give up in bewilderment as the situation seems to get more hopelessly entangled, for the Thread of Life sometimes gets snarled, but with patience and care it can be straightened out. Good night, my dearest ones, and God be with you.''

—Caladar Ramonsara
From: The newsbooklet—'Universarius'

"Legion Of Stars"

''Until such time, know that you are watched over, that you are constantly in our thoughts and on our monitors, and none of you walk alone for you walk with the 'Legion Of The Stars' at your side.''
Received by Tuieta

—Monka

CHAPTER THREE

THE FLIGHT

OF THE

EAGLES

PHOTO BY KEVIN LAHEY

PHOTO BY MARCUS

"Welcome Their Arrival"

"We have begun to bring ones of our planets and galaxies to your Earth to assist you. These dear ones have been taken to various parts of Earth to help you. They come as ones like you, though they have full knowledge of their purpose.

Many of them are schooled in the higher teachings given by the celestial hierarchy. They have reached the balance and harmony of the universe and they come to share with you the teachings they have received and to help you achieve your measure of peace and harmony.

I ask that each of you in your hearts welcome their arrival and you would share your light for their safety."
Received by Tuieta **—Andromeda Rex**

"Eagles Gathering"

"For there are Eagles gathering in that great land, and their great wisdom, entity, are going to impart wondrous things to the world and it will coincide, entity, with things coming outside of the world."
Channeled by J.Z. Knight **—Ramtha**

"Forerunners of Peace"

"It has been said that there shall be trying times, and it is so. While it is given unto 'them' to run amuck, I say unto thee: Hold ye firm, keep thine feet firmly planted upon the Rock which shall be unto thee thine sure foundation, and it shall not fail thee.

Bless them which are the forerunners of Peace, for they shall be as the ones sent that they might partake in the work at hand, that they might help establish a New Order, and that

they might be within the place they are prepared for yet greater things.

Let thine hearts be filled with Love and Compassion for them, and give thanks that they are come, for theirs is no small part.

Ye shall stand up this day and be counted. Whom servest thou? Answer ye Me—whom servest thou? This is the day in which ye answer. Call unto the Light, and ye shall be heard. *Ye shall seek the Light.* Walk ye in *it* and be ye as one prepared for greater things. So let it be as The Father has willed it.
—I AM the Most Worthy Grand Master of the
Recorded by Sister Thedra **—Inner Temple**

"Our Volunteers"

"Those of you who have come at this hour to assist the others of Earth are indeed on a mission of Love and Mercy. It is by your own choice that you have come—volunteered. Just as we of the Fleet have volunteered for our roles here, so it is in the case of you ones on Earth.

There are ones of you that have come from distant planets, stars, galaxies, and universes. Each of you have volunteered to come to assist those that are Earth bound, to rise up from their bondage. It is our unending joy when we can

Note: The preceeding photo was taken during the First Annual Gathering of the Children of Light, which took place on the side of Mt. Shasta right below where you see the craft. That is 'if' you do *see* this materialization of Our Brothers Crystalline Vehicle?!

89

make contact with one of 'our volunteers.' I will also add a note to this fact and it is that each one that is on Earth has come on a particular mission. Just as each of us here has a particular role or assignment, so it is with you dear ones embodied on Earth at this hour.

There are many, many that volunteered to come, and once they have entered the ethers of Earth they have been lost to their purpose. They have been caught in the web of Earth, and so far we have been unable to help them to break loose, for they have expressed no real desire to be loosed from the web. You see we cannot intercede if that is not the choice of the one on Earth, even if this one is come on a particular assignment from the Confederation. We have to replace that one or ask of another in embodiment to assume the additional assignment. In some cases we can ask of several ones to share of the one assignment so that their load will not be too heavy.

But my message this hour is not to speak of those ones that have chosen to reject their assignment but rather to give a 'well done O' Faithful ones' to each of you that has begun to assume your assignment. Some of you will go forth during this total period and not feel that you are fully cognizant as to your purpose or your objective. You are ones that are guided by a 'hunch' or intuition. This is our mode of operation with you for this particular time. This is the mode of operation that we will be using with large numbers of ones that are working within the Light. So many of you cry for direct communication with us or with ones of the angelic realms. You are in constant contact with us but it may not be in the mode of your own choice. Long before you came to this land it was your mode of choice. As the hour draws closer the communication will be sharpened and clarified.

Each of you has a specific purpose that is unlike that of your neighbor. Awaken to your purpose and to your assignment. Alert yourself to your inner guidance and all that is is available for you. I shall close of this hour. Be at peace and be filled with the love that is abundantly shared with you. Adonai   Peace   Vassau   Vassau
Received by Tuieta — **Monka**

"Intense Light Activity"

"Those of you who serve in your places, be assured that all who participate in this program know you are there! It is beautiful to behold these beams of Light, as one looks down upon the planet from our ships high above you in orbit. A similar projection also is in evidence in locations of intense Light activity, such as meetings, seminars, etc."
Received by Tuella — **Ashtar**

"Many Voices Will Be Raised"

"I speak on behalf of the entire Spiritual Hierarchy when I plead with you to realize that 'time is short,' and whatever thou wouldst do toward spiritual expansion had best be done quickly. The coming onslaught will bring with it the end of materialistic dreams and objectionable goals.

The inner planetary expulsions will soon be felt and be seen in an outward manifestation upon the surface of the land. As these things come to pass, many voices will be raised, and many great works will be seen, such as have never been seen. These will be the works of these who have been lifted into our midst, from whom the veils have been removed, and whose chakras have been fully opened. Souls who see them and hear them will know that these anointed ones have truly been with us and returned with a witness and the evidence that cannot be denied. For a 'brief moment of time' their ministries will be blessed and protected, and they shall no longer be secluded away without freedom of service. They shall stand boldly in many places, witnessing to the experiences that come to them in higher realms, where they were given a full insight to the events that are just before the world. When they have been raised in your midst, listen to these voices!"

Received by Tuella   **—Lord Kuthumi**

"When It Is Come— The Hour For the 'Servers' To Come Forth"

"Be they saint or sinner they are subject unto the same law—the law under which they have come to serve—for each comes into the Earth under the law—each earthborn come under the law of Earth—each born of woman. It is said that the ones born of woman are bound by the laws of Earth—while the ones which are not born of woman are exempt from such laws. Yet these come under the Law of the Confederacy—they are subject to the law of the realm unto which they belong.

They come into the Earth as in bodies of flesh—liken unto the Earthling (and he has the right) for he uses the law for the good of all—he comes with the Galactic Law—none conflict. For it is given unto the Galactic Confederacy to know the law governing all the realms within its jurisdiction—and it is said they all operate within and with the consent of the Federation—the Brotherhoods are all one with the Confederation—with the Great and Mighty Council. The Twentyfour Elders are one with the Confederacy—they sit in Council with the ones which are yet over them—for it is ever so—that there are other Councils to which the lesser looks for counsel—yet this is the work of the Galactic Council, to give of certain help—assistance (Light) at this time that the Earth and her children be lifted up.

When it is come that the hour strikes for the 'Servers' to come forth and make themselves known—they shall know each and every one which is prepared to give of themselves in selfless service—for this shall be required of them in that day—when the great wave of darkness shall precede the onrush of Great Light.

I say: The days of darkness shall precede the onrush of Great Light.

Such Light is now being released—yet not in its fullness for they could not bear it—and it is not yet time for them to be removed from the Earth—it is not yet time!

While it is come that certain things are being done in preparation for the great onrush of darkness and Light—it is the law that We wait the time wherein certain action shall take place.

It is said that they first shall be warned—prepared and ready. To the ones which have not heeded the warnings We say: *'Thou hast been warned'* so be it that We have done Our part.

Yet I say: The warnings shall be many—and some violent in nature—they shall see and hear the Hand of God move—I say they shall see and hear—for it shall move! and none shall stay it!—for the Earth shall go through great and violent changes—and the children shall be therein the recipients of such action. The effects thereof shall be unto some unbearable—yet is is said: "Be ye as ones prepared—put on the whole Armor of God and no harm shall come nigh unto thee!

Recorded by Sister Thedra

91

"Soon the Eagles Shall be Summoned"

"Soon the eagles shall be summoned, and we shall begin our part of the final days. There are many who question if they are of the eagles, but I say to each, you will know as your time approaches. To all who seek and question, I say that the light of each of you is vital to all of those on Mother Earth, for you are presently her balance and her strength. There is much need on the part of each of you to hold fast, and grow in the Light as never before. Know, dear ones, that you are watched-over, and never shall you be lost or forsaken. I grieve that all of mankind cannot and is not as stalwart as each of you.

I send love and greetings from all of us to each of you.
Received by Tuieta   —**I AM Monka** signing off this hour.

"Missionaries from Space"

"The Eagles, 'missionaries from space,' who are to receive these messages, will be surprised at both the variety and importance of their final assignments. The leaders of this final work will emerge from those of you who have quietly prepared in this lifetime for the fulfillment of visions and destinies they have known they are working for. Each wave of vibrational turning up that has been accomplished on this planet has brought forth spiritual leaders who effected and supported these spiritual advancements through writings, teachings, music, arts, drama, inventions, science, etc. Like a surfer emerging on the crest, their voices and influence has been spiritually uplifting to humanity. Now, as this fall progresses, will come forward the last wave cresting as it sweeps o're the planet."
Received by Lyara   —**Commander Jycondria**

"Listen Eagles"

"Listen Eagles: I am here to discuss the question that comes so often to the Light Workers. So many souls still involve themselves in the dates and such, pertinent to their lifting. Although it was explained in our book that no dates could be given, I repeat again that which so many have clearly explained who serve me, that dates will not be given!

We are not fortune tellers. We see processes set in motion, energies gathering and gaining momentum; we observe changes weaving their pattern in situation. However, no member of our Commands nor of the Spiritual Hierarchy can give mankind a certain date, and should such be done, then use much caution and discernment concerning it, for this is not in harmony with things as they are.

The will of man collectively, events upon the planet, and the possible progression and advancement of the Light as well as the darkness—are all involved in the details of events that would lead to the lifting up and the gathering of the Eagles, as well as the full phases of an evacuation of the planet of the remnant. The importance that must be stressed is not the moment in time, but the preparation for that moment, on the soul level. This is where the emphasis must be placed and is where it will continue to be placed. For one who is totally ready and qualified, there is no need for dates to be given until the very moment has come. Howbeit, in no instance will individuals be given long periods of notice for readiness, but only short notices would be given, for security purposes.

I would ask that this be passed along to the Light workers: Not to seek for a setting of time, but for a thankfulness of an extension of time in which to spread more Light throughout the planet thus to prepare may others. This is the call and the mission, to 'occupy' until He comes Who must come!"
Received by Tuella   —**Ashtar**

92

PHOTO BY ZENON MICHALAK

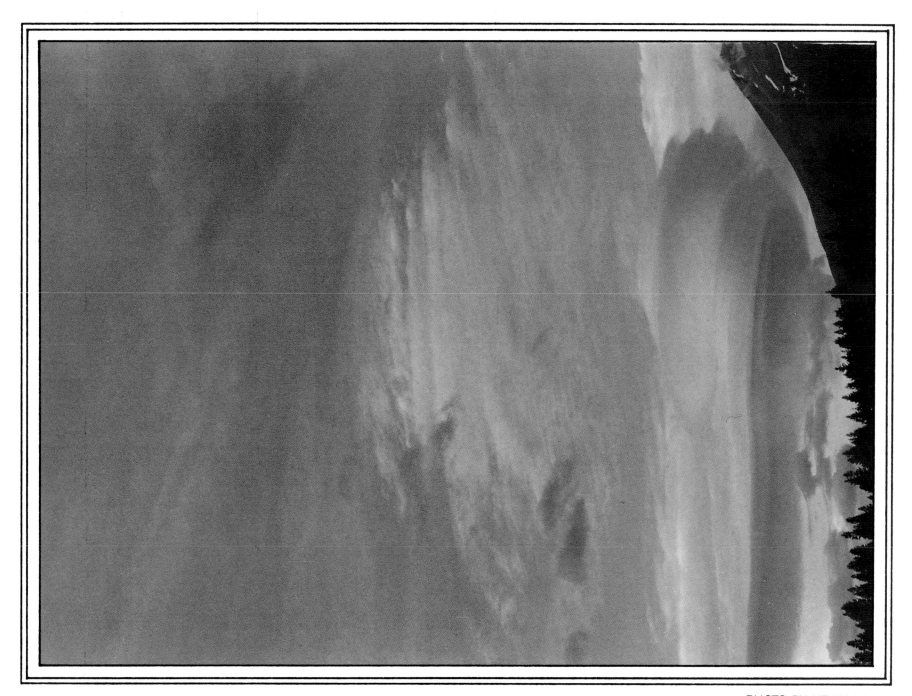

PHOTO BY KEVIN LAHEY

PHOTO BY KEVIN LAHEY

"As The Winged Eagle"

"Sori, Sori—Mighty is the hand of God—Swift is the hand of the Almighty *One*.

I am come that ye see the hand move in all its swiftness and surety, for with swiftness and surety it moveth. It passeth over the Earth as The Winged Eagle; It passeth over the Seas and the land as the mighty fortress, and it bringeth peace unto the initiated. Yet unto the uninitiated it might bring great fear and foreboding, for its power is felt by the un-initiated; and knowing not that which is felt, they fear. Yet I say unto thee, fear not, for I am come that this day be fulfilled.

I am come that this day be the fulfillment of all past ages. So be it this day shall bring forth the Gold from the Crucilbe, in its radiant purity, and nothing shall contaminate it, neither shall it be destroyed any more—it shall be as nothing known unto man in ages past. I am come that man be liberated from his bondage.

I am come!   I AM come!   *I AM come!*
Watch!   See!   Know!   For this am I *come!*
Watch!   See!   Know!   For this am I *come!*"

Recorded by Sister Thedra   **—Sananda**

"Be You Like A Great Eagle"

"When you can't find joy in all your life and laugh at your illusions and own em', you're the living dead. You never know the beauty of silver wings in the height of day, you never know the beauty of the fiery jewel in the east in an early morning. You never know the crying of night birds, you never know a gentle breeze in your hair. You never know the wind on the water and you never become the golden color of leaves in the spice of autumn. You never know the beauty of a crackling fire with alder/pine and the sweet smells and the light dancing in flames putting on a virtual play for you. You never know the essence of a room filled with smells of leather and wood and books and dust, draperies and animals. You don't know that! You don't know to sit on a high mountain and to be caught up in the breath of forever in the availability to *see* forever. *Be you like a great eagle* where there is no man to torment you, or to bring you down, but just to *be*. You don't know what it is to ride a black steed with hoofs of fire and nostrils of flame, and the mane within your face, and the power beneath your legs over rollings hills. You don't know what it is to put your face into the grasses of spring, *you don't know!!!* And you say you've lived! You don't know what it is to contemplate the enchantress in the stars, you don't know what it is to be up all night and to watch the waxing and the waning of that silvery beauty or to see golden rods of sunrise pierce the misty mountains deep in a purple hue, *you don't know! You haven't lived!!* You have been the living dead because all that was ever important was what you worked!, rather than what you *are*."

Channeled by J.Z. Knight   **—Ramtha**

"I Cover You With My Golden Cloak"

"I am Kuthumi, World Teacher, and my own emanations and vibrations surround every world volunteer at this hour. I cover you with my Golden Cloak, and I charge your being on inner levels to hold fast to your crown and to steadfastly remain faithful to your pledge. Realize that a great cloud of powerful Beings surrounds you and exalts your calling and giveth you grace equal to the task. Others who speak after me will introduce the details of our plan. I shed forth my love and blessing to all who have determined to serve as 'ground forces' in this tremendous undertaking."

Received by Tuella   **—Kuthumi**

"Come Up As The Eagle"

"Mine Children: This day I would say unto thee, arise and soar with Me—come up as the eagle; be ye as ones rested upon the mountain top—let not thine opinions thine preconceived ideas bind thee unto the valley—the shadows. I say unto thee, the shadows are the unrealitites, while the mountain top forever is the mountain top. Let not the shadows frighten thee—neither offend thee, for I say unto thee, they shall pass as nothing and be no more—they shall be remembered no more—so be it that I am come that it be so.

I come that the unreality shall pass—that ye shall come to know the reality, so let it be. For this do I say unto thee, let not the unreality frighten thee. Be ye as ones steadfast; rest in the knowing that I AM. The Lord thy God has spoken that ye might be so prepared for the greater part—which is reality.

Recorded by Sister Thedra   **—I AM Sananda**

CHAPTER FOUR

ENLIGHTENMENT

THROUGH
THE POWER
OF

SPIRIT

"He Must Make of His Choice—Once Every 26,000 Years"

"Now be ye at peace and kno ye it is Michael that does speak. May the peace of the Divine One abide within you as you go forth. It is that man has cum to that portion of the cycle that is of the closing and man is of that time of the cycle when he must make his choice—whether to cum forward or to stay. He must make of his choice. Once every 26,000 years must he make of his decision. It is at that time now that the choice must be made. It is not of the time to wait or to dawdle along the path. Such an attitude will cause you to be left by the wayside as the others cum into the next dimension. It is that you of this plane must prepare and be earnest in your preparation if you are to achieve the next dimension."

Received by Tuieta   **—Archangel Michael**

"What Is Your Fuel?—Who Are You?"

"You have heard of the Masters. Do you think people become Masters because they do not know who they are? Do you think you can take courses to find out who you are or any kind of teaching? Not so. Not so, my children. Move along to a clearer perception of who you are. If you have machinery, you go to plug it in; you got to have right plug, male/female. You got gasoline engine, you got to know it's gasoline; you got kerosene, you got to know the fuel. Now you are a spiritual engine. You were made to do work. What is your fuel? Who are you?"

From the newsletter publication 'Lightlines'   **—Yada**

"All Men Are Capable of Cosmic Communication"

"The power of thought is said to have no limitations or boundaries. Can you build a wall around the thought of a man? You know that you cannot. Thought is as expansive as the universe itself. Therefore, still the body, quiet the mind, and think on us, and we will respond to those who do in love turn thoughts toward us of the Intergalactic Space Confederation.

All men are capable of cosmic communication. All of humanity is mentally endowed sufficiently to manifest the aspects of the fully opened mind. The human brain is fully adequate to operate in all of its capacity in all of its inherent functions of sensory perceptions beyond that of the physical senses. There is no paradox here. There is no mystery involved. We are discussing a natural phenomenon not in any way religious, nor superstitious, nor that which must be hidden in the archives of old philosophies. This natural ability is within the scope of all mankind, and not merely by a gifted few.

The inability of humanity to exercise these divine talents lies in their own misguided concepts and not in their limitations. All of mind is placed at their disposal, requiring only conscious cooperation of the human consciousness.

The spiritual essence of soul-mind is the key to realization of the fullest potential within the human lifespan. Mentally speaking, mankind is still crawling on all fours, when they are capable of walking tall in the gait of the conqueror. The awakening of the resonating center of the human brain could deliver the earthean society from self-imposed limitations, if they would but apply themselves to these concepts."

Received by Tuella   **—Ashtar**

"P-O-W-A-H"

"We shall speak this night of that which is an elusive thing to you of your plane, of your dimension. For we shall speak of powah, P-O-W-A-H, powah. Know you what this is? Nay, me thinks you think I have difficulty with my speech. Not so. For this powah, is greater than that which you kno as power. See I have not difficulty with my tongue. Know you what power is? Upon your plane you see power as the mighty machine that moves great hills of soil, of dirt. Or you see explosions of your bombs, and your missiles, and you call this power. Or you speak of ones who have great wealth, great stores, and they play of others as puppets upon strings. And you say this is power. Or you look at your rivers and as they are dammed up and the waters are held back so can they bring forth great power. All of these you call as power, all of these are manifestations of this upon your plane.

But let us speak of powah. Know you that you could stand with your feet planted firmly upon this sphere called Earth, and you could hold up your hand, and you could command that a star would sit in your hand. And then you might release it. Or you could sit beneath the shade of a great and mighty tree, and you could call to the birds and they would rest upon your finger. And you could speak to the animals of the field, and they would cum and they would sit with you, and they would tell you of the mysteries that they know. This is possible, my lords, this is possible. Within you this day this is possible. Yes, you have but to recognize who you are, and desire, and the manifestation of your desire is there.

You have at the tips of your fingers the ability to travel of the stars with no machines, with no conveyances. This is powah. Of a distant day this you did, and it was quite ordinary, quite ordinary. And you had at-one-ment, and you had balance, and you had harmony, and you had peace. And this was enfolded in the love which was your creation. For you see when you came unto this plane, when you came forth before you even came unto this plane, you were given all the Lord God of Totality manifested. Not-thing, no thing was kept from you, for you were from the seed of the Lord God of Totality. And as he sent you forth he gave to you all that he was, that he is, he ever will be. And he said, 'Manifest this of Me.' Thy Divine Creator had no intent for you to grovel in the ground. You were placed to manifest what you truly are. And of these eons you have had a slowing in your evolution, and I merely speak to awaken that which is within you, that perfect portion, your powah.

To say the word brings forth great air from the lungs— powah, wah—the breath of life, the breath of Creation. Ponder of this. Cut away that which encapsulates you into a specific dimension. For you are more than that, you are much more than that. It is time that you recognized this. You have groveled and you have looked to others to give you answers. You have looked to others to tell you what to do, when to do, and how to do it. And you have looked to others to give you magic potions that will give you the communion with the other dimensions. And you have said, "Surely, if I turn around three times, for this is what they do, then I shall be as they are. Or surely if I sleep with a certain rock beneath my pillow.'

Beloved one, you have within you, you have the powah, the breath of creation, you have this within you. You have within you the ability to stop the rain, to call forth the rainbow, this is yours. You need no magic potion. You need to recognize, who you are, what you are, and why you are. For you are the powah, the breath of life. You are the manifestation of the Divine Essence, the Perfect. The Lord God of Totality has placed within you, the Divine Essence which is the Lord God of your being. And you have within you the breath which is the Creative Force. Is this not a most wondrous gift? Is this not a most wondrous realization? Come

PHOTO BY MICHAEL ZANGER

PHOTO BY KEVIN LAHEY

ye forth in at-one-ment with that which you truly are. Leave of the pettiness, of the smallness, of the insignificant, leave of these things, and come forth to your own beauty, to your own attunement, and at-one-ment, at-one-ment. This is to recognize who you are, what you are, and why you are, and to be the sum total of your own totality. And as you are the sum total of your own Totality, so can the Lord God of your totality, that Divine Essence which came forth at the Beginning, make of its own realization upon your plane And so shall you then recognize of your own powah.

In many times, in many ways have I spoken with you, and each time I have said to you—you are beautiful, you are as none other in the total of all the Cosmos, for you are unique. You are your own star, you are your own shining crystal, you are your own light. For you see, the Lord God of Totality did not believe in your, as you would say, assembly line production. Each that has been sent forth has come as a unique gift. You have been told this. Each time that I did speak with you I have spoken of this. I have said to you of your worth, of your beauty, of your purpose. I have said to you to be, be all that you can be, now—not of the morrow, or the day after, or the day after, but now. Be all that you can be.

Know you why I did come forth at this hour to speak with you? I will tell you. This has been a period for you ones of your dimension that has been a period of great cleansing, of purging, of self searching. It has been a time of emotional upheaval. It has been a time when many ones have been brought to their knees. It has been a period within your individual growth that you have felt quite lowly. And yes, as things have come forth up to the surface, you have felt quite ashamed. And so it is the Great Council that did gather has sent ones forth to let you know that you are releasing a great deal of garbage, that it might be neutralized, so to speak, and used in a more useful manner.

I have come, as others have come, thru other ones, to let you know that as you have gone through each of these experiences, as you are tested, as you have been tried, as you have wept at your own frailties—that you are loved, that you are beautiful, that you are unique, that you are most wondrous. I have spoken to you of that which you are capable of doing that I might lift your eye from the mundane, from the purging that you are experiencing, that you might see beyond this to that which you truly are, that you might see why you are experiencing the purging. I have come to help you to see beyond your immediate experience. Oh, you have read, and some of you know partially of your purpose and that which you must do. And you amassed a certain amount of knowing upon your plane. But all of this has not prepared you for the feelings, for the experiences that you have experienced, And yes, beloved brethren, you shall experience these until the next full moon. And so at that time shall you feel a measure of release from this.

I have come to offer to you reason, to help you to see purpose for that which you are experiencing. In a word, I have tried to help you to clear your eye so that you might see the rainbow, even though you hear the thunder, and see the lightning. Yes, this has been my purpose, and to share of my love, for I love you. Each one of you, I love you. I love that which you truly are. And I recognize of your aches and your hurts and your cries, for I have walked of the same steps, I have traveled of the same steps, And I have cried, and I have ached, and I have cast my eye up, and I have looked for a measure that I might see beyond that which I was experiencing. And it came. Ones came, and they helped me and they sustained me, and they gave me courage and they gave me strength to continue along this narrow, narrow, narrow road that you must walk. And so I come to give you strength, to give you encouragement, to offer a measure of comfort for what you are experiencing.

Now there are many ones that shall come to you and they shall say that the sunshine will be always, that there will be no rain clouds. And I say to you, how will the grain grow if you have no rain? How will you grow if you have no tests? How will you rise above something if you have nothing to rise above? For as you realize of your tests, as you realize of your trial and you overcome this one, and you stay along that narrow, narrow road so does the powah within you grow, so does it grow. Can you not feel this within your breast?

Many ones have traveled of this path, and as it grows narrow they fall to the wayside. Know you that you are never asked to travel of this path alone, for ones will always be with you to assist you along this path. And so I have come to assist you. I want you to come forth, and as I say, I want you to come forth, the Lord God which is me, the Lord God which I am, which is of the Lord God of Totality, calls to you to come that you might recognize true attunement and at-one-ment. My beautiful brethren, I await you. Om ni di eno

Received by Tuieta   —**Theoaphylos**

"They Have The Power To Do That But So Do You!"

"Your Higher brothers that are in your space ships as you call them—the only difference between them and you is that they have activated greater parts of their seat of receivership but they're in the same knowingness as you are, the only difference has been that they are doing something about it. They have the ability to transform their bodies however they need to, to suit whatever—whatever pore or whatever radius they are entering into. They have the power to do that but *so do you!* and *never* fantasize yourself that they are coming here to do away with you or captivate you or to carry you off to some place for you have not earned the right to 'be carried off'* yet.

Channeled by J.Z. Knight   —**Ramtha**
(* 'be carried off'= spacetravel)

"The Telepathic Thread"

"We have taught those who thus 'hear' us, through long and tedious training sessions of sitting quietly with us, to become receivers of our transmissions. With some, such an ability has to be developed. With others it was present within at birth. Regardless, it is a fact that humankind is perfectly proficient of pure telepathy of the highest level of clarity and perception.

Let us then accept the validity of the process and consider the fruit of it. Our mental conversations with our messengers are as real as your conversations with anyone you know or love or meet. The telepathic thread of experiencing soundless words within the mind is a lucid and fluent as your own tongue."

Received by Tuella   —**Ashtar**

"Silence"

"Beloved of Mine Being: This day I would say unto thee: Be ye alert, and fortune thineself the part of wisdom, for I say unto thee: The Silence which is necessary unto thine learning is of great importance. No word can convey unto that which can be imparted unto thee thru silence. I say, silence is of great importance unto Us, for in the silence can We reach thee—be ye as ones prepared, and for this do I speak of silence.

While it is given unto thee to communicate thru the spoken word, it is give unto thee to hear that which we say unto thee, with thine inner ear. So be it that We speak unto thee in words which are not heard by the outer ear—it is of a different frequency, and not audible unto thee, when thou are speaking. Silence is the key which hast to be turned, for Us to enter in thru thine door. Be ye blest this day."

—I AM thine Brother and thine Sibor, **BOR**
Recorded by Sister Thedra

" 'Enlightened '—It is One Who Does Not Have A Closed Mind"

Enlightenment means, to be 'in Light of' knowledge, *knowledge.* Knowledge, as it were indeed, is that which takes one from that which is termed his boarders, to an unlimited expanse. Knowledge it is that which unlimits the mind, it is that which gratifies the body, it is that which defies death, it is Knowledge. So if one is that which is termed enlightened, it is one who does not have a closed mind. Knowledge, as it were indeed, has been known to be very frightening, know why? Because there are many entities who have their own opinion of how things should be, and enlightenment challenges that opinion and takes away their identity—because their opinion constitutes their identity.

Now let me tell you how it will work, once one desires this, wonderful thing happens in the physical body—this (third eye area) begins to open up, it is like a — it looks like a little pear, then the mouth begins to bloom—it opens up and begins to look like a flower. How ridiculous they have called it another eye, it doesn't resemble an eye at all, it resembles a flower. It is called the pituitary systems, heard you of it?

Then as it begins to open, it secrets a hormone flow that flows into the brain into the pineal system that sits here (near the back of the brain). The pineal system is then activated and it begins to open up another part of the brain, you see? This is a receiver (the brain), it does not create thought it only receives it. So the thoughts that are coming in through conscious level come in through the auric field. So you are being bombarded as it were with thought propellents, they look like straight line rays of Light, very swift. The little receiver in here, can only pick up those sections of thought that are in alignment with it's capability to receive them and then transmit them through the physiological body. If you have *brilliance,* or *genius,* or that which is termed outrageous thoughts and they come into you and there is no place for them to be received—you see you never get it!!! You see?

Now once another phase of this wondrous receiver is activated then it can elevate itself to pick up the higher frequencies. Once the higher frequencies come into your receiver they are transmitted through that which is termed the spinal system. know you what that is? It is the spark that gives each cell life and allows it to duplicate itself, so it rejuvenates life—and the overall sensation of that is recorded in the soul. And it is in the soul that it stores it as emotion and that which is termed the intellectual mind deciphers it and then says that is what the feeling is. Genius or that which is termed enlightenment has no memory here (soul). So when you begin to be enlightened, you begin to be dizzy. You begin, to be light in your head and then you begin to get sensations of feelings and you don't know how to describe them. And they come into the soul and the soul registers a New Emotion. And you beget more and more of them. The collectiveness of that begins to aspire you to communicate it—and show you things you saw before with a limited mind no longer applies but the limited mind opens up to express the unlimited mind. You *see? You change,* because you feel differently now. That is how it All works, in enlightenment one presses to allow, *allow, ALLOW!* The more you allow the more you activate that center to open that frequency, it is very scientific. And the more you go with what you feel and listen to what you feel, it is a signal emerges in the body to allow the whole to open up and I could cut your arm off and you would say *"I will* grow another" and within moments you would have another one appear. It is called miracle, but it belongs to You, it *is* called *God.*

Whenever you feel this master, say: "From the Lord God of my Being I accept it, I accept it, I accept it *indeed!'*

Now, know you what the **Lord God of your Being** *is???* Really!!!, know you that that which is termed the poorest of teachers teach philosophically and the poor wretched creatures that have come to learn know only how to repeat, and have no understanding of what it means at *all!!!* They're very unenlightened! So to be most prudent and wise, Entity, in your adventure ask what it is your asking. So that you can identify it!

The **Lord** of your being is the Soul, it weighs thirteen ounces, it is that which keeps all of this together when you are off somewhere else. It is the Soul that is the child of the Spirit, without it you could not occupy thought within your being.

Now what is the giver of Life? It is the **God** of your being, that is the spirit, it is that which encompasses all that you are and allows for all the thought to come.

The **Being** is the totality of what you are that connects you with all that there is, so the Lord—God—of your Being is in harmony with all that is.

So you have addressed everything within your being and it listens when you address it. It will become in focus. You see, you are very complex and yet you are very simple, and *you are* very beautiful. Address it, it'll hear you because it is a Lord, a God, an Entity, a Master that speaks. And when you tell it to remember it will remember, when you tell it to erase it will erase, if you tell it to be greater it will be *greater,* very simple!

Don't forget another important thing, Love what you are. You never harm it, never lie to it, never abuse it, Love what you are it *is* worth loving.
Channeled by J.Z. Knight   **—Ramtha**

"Pity is the One Which Knows Not The Power of the Spirit"

"Sori Sori—Behold ye the Plan, seek ye knowledge of the Way of Life. Light shall be shed upon the secrets of Life, and none shall keep from thee that which is thine by inheritance, for it is endowed unto thee of The Eternal Father. So be it I speak unto thee of the mysteries of Life—each as a part of the Whole. So be it that the Whole is made up of many parts, divisions, even as the body of man is made up of many cells, limbs, and parts yet unnamed. Ye shall come to see the body of man as a lesser symbol of the Eternal Father—yet He resembles not the form of man, for He is not a man—*He is the All,* The First, The Last, the totality of the *all,* The *whole,* without beginning, without end. So be it We call this *all 'He,'* for the Name is that which is not spoken—save by the breath—not by the tongue is it spoken. Therein is the Mystery of the First—the breath which is not of the earthly substance, but of the Spirit. The Spirit dwelleth in flesh, yet it is not bound in flesh. It causeth flesh to be, for the breath of God moveth upon the ETH, and flesh comes into life and Animates that which is seen as dense flesh. Pity is the one which knows not the power of Spirit, for he is fortuned to be as one blind and deaf; he is called the 'walking dead,' for he is amongst the dead."
Recorded by Sister Thedra   **—Sananda**

PHOTO BY KEVIN LAHEY

PHOTO BY KEVIN LAHEY

"Awakening Their Capabilities Gradually"

"Science speaks of inversion or repulsion as an opposing force. So it is that there is a negative and a postive force ever pulsating through the channels of Mind in the inflow and outflow of atoms of energy and their reaction upon the human brain cells. Positive action flows through the pineal doorway, while negative* action flows through the pituitary doorway, both reacting in unison in the balancing of all the activity of the mental faculties.

As the world stands waiting to learn of telepathic abilities, the glands of the human form will be injected with powerful rays and influence from outer space which will expand the abilities of the pituitary and pineal glands, awakening their capabilities gradually, throughout society."

Received by Tuella   **—Aljanon**

(*negative—this has no connotation of judgement, but merely is a term used to describe a balance of polarity)

"Moving Into A New State of Consciousness"

"Suns of Light, rapid changes are occurring on Planet Earth in preparation for the advent of the 'New' Age of *Light*. These changes are observed both on the physical level and on the spiritual level. Many transformations are going on, on the surface of the Planet—weather changes affecting both land and sea, slight deviations of the world's axis, and atmospheric changes. None of this must alarm a Pure Sun of Light for you must remember that all is in Divine Order and nothing transpires which is not for the ultimate *good* of the planet and of the *total universe*.

Spiritually there are also many changes as well as 'new' attitudes being adopted. Unquestionably the Divine Will is also Master of these changes—that is why you are observing certain groups in their downfall while others appear to be progressing. We speak here primarily of the 'New Age' Groups rather than the 'Old Age' religious organizations. At this time in history the realm of Light is impressing the pure Consciousness of 'man' with a discriminating mind in order to 'sift' out the false ideas from the true ones—whenever a Planet experiences an active period in it's history, as Earth is now doing, the dual forces must show the dark as well as the Light, as each one learns to discriminate between the two. My Suns it is *so* important for each of you to discover your own Inner Guidance and not depend solely on the Realm of Light to decide things for you. We can be with you, We can inspire you—but you—your Expressive Self must make the final judgement regarding the true and the false."

—I AM THAT I AM—Light—Love—Life of the Universe
From 'New Age Teachings'

"Into the New Age of Aquarius"

"This is the voice of Gramaha, the representative of the Ashtar Command, speaking to you.

For many years now you have seen us as Lights in the skies. We speak to you now in Peace and Wisdom as we have done to your Brothers and Sisters all over this, your Planet Earth. We come to warn you of the Destiny of your Race and your Worlds so that you may communicate to your fellow Beings the course you must take to avoid the disasters which threaten your Worlds, and the Beings on our Worlds around you. This is in order that you may share in the great awakening, as the Planet passes into the New Age of Aquarius. The New Age can be a time of great Peace and Evolution for your Race, but only if your Rulers are made aware of the evil forces that can overshadow their judgements.

Be still now and listen, for your chance may not come again. For many years your Scientists, Governments and Generals have not heeded our warnings; they have continued to experiment with the evil forces of what you call nuclear energy. Atomic bombs can destroy the Earth, and the Beings of your Sister Worlds, in a moment. The wastes from the Atomic Power Systems will poison your Planet for many thousands of your years to come. We, who have followed the path of Evolution far longer than you, have long since realized this—that Atomic Energy is always directed against Life. It has no Peaceful application. Its use, and research into its use, must be ceased at once, or you all risk destruction.

You have but a short time to learn to live together in Peace and Goodwill. Small Groups over the the Planet are learning this, and exist to pass on the Light of the dawning New Age to you all. You are free to accept or reject their teachings, but only those who learn to live in Peace will pass to the higher realms of spiritual evolution.

Have no fears, seek only to know yourselves and live in Harmony with the ways of your planet Earth.

We of the Ashtar Galactic Command thank you for your attention. We are now leaving the planes of your existence. May you be Blessed by the Supreme Love and Truth of the Cosmos.

(The above communication was reprinted from New Life Magazine, *London, who managed to obtain an unpublished transcript of the 'voice intervention' from Outer Space which occurred on Southern Television in the Hannington area at 5:05 p.m. on Saturday, 26th of November 1977.)*

"Today's Answers?!!"

"Your Earth is moving into a new 'octave of existence' . . . The days of miracles are here. Today's answers will not be found in your University textbooks. The answers will come from an extension of your knowing, a re-awakening from within. Blessed Ones . . . your minds will and must go ahead. In this 'lower arc' you live in a world of 'gravity' . . . but as you ascend to the 'Higher Arcs', you will find the 'realm of Levity.' And when you open that 'individual forcefield' many things will happen."

Recorded by KaRene   —**Alon** . . . Love & Blessings

"Kno You How You Got Here?"

"Greetings, myne brethren. Think ye that I had forsook thee? Nay, this not so. And now it is at this hour that the Lord God of my being comes forth to stand with the Lord God of thy being, that we might lift our voice, our thot in one great form to the Lord God of Totality. Tis Theoaphylos that does speak. I bid thee greetings. I bid thee peace. I bid thee joy. And I would pose to thee a question of this hour.

Kno you how you got here? Ah, and you say to me you were the gleam in your father's eye, and you were the giggle that was upon your mother's lips, that's how you got here. I say, partly, partly this I say. Before that time when ye did come into this place, before you had a thot, before you had a form that was your own, the Lord God of Totality thot. He thot, and he thot you. Know you are a thot made manifest. It is so, for that is what you are. That is what creation is. It is a thot made manifest. And just as you are a thot made manifest, so be the tree, and the bird, and the flower and the blade of grass. For each, for all of creation began as the thot brought forth. From the Divine Mind, the Divine Will, came forth the thot, and the thot was sent forth to manifest, as was given by the Lord God of Totality. Ponder of this I say.

Then you ask of me, 'Brethren, what of my vehicle (body) then?' Tis a thot also, a thot made manifest. Look about you. Look about you I say. All that which you see, which you touch, which you taste, which you smell, which you feel, which you are, is thot made manifest. Condensed if you will. For upon your plane thot is this airy something that sits above you—as your comic strip with it's clouds of balloons that have words in them. This is thot. All which is, is thot manifest. Can you begin to grasp how total this is, how great this is, this thot, this gift, this ability? Thot, thot, think, think, and *be*.

Now if you are thot manifest from the Divine Principle then you are of the Divine Principle, and you are God. You are our Lord God. And have you not the ability to think, to have thot? Tis so. But what do you do with it, what do you do I ask? You think—do my shoes match my stockings, or should I part my hair on the other side of my head, or what shall I prepare for breakfast, or what shall I put upon the grocery list, and what shall I say to this one that slighted me, or what shall I do for this one that has brought me such joy. These are your thots, these are your thoughts, are they not? Tsk Tsk Tsk.

Thot is creation, thot is creating. You are thot, you are a creator. You think. So what do you manifest, what have you manifested with your thots? Have you manifested a rose, or have you created a concerto, or have you thot a building into being? Have you, have you healed another with a thot of love, of perfectness, of balance within that one? You do not hold on to your thots long enough to do anything with them. Your thoughts travel at the speed of light so quickly do they leave you, and you're on to other ones. You do not stop your thinking process long enough at this point to manifest much of anything but chaos. Know you what chaos is? Chaos is confusion, it is unbalance, it is a heaviness in the wrong direction. This is chaos.

Do you recognize that you have this within you? Yes, you can think a flower to bloom. You can build a most magnificent building in your thots. And if you would hold that thot, truly you could manifest of that. You could think of yourself in another city, and as you would hold of this thot of this place, of this city where you wish to be, you could be there. So great is the power of thot, so great is your power of thot.

Oh, beloved brethren, my small brethren, use that which you have. It is most delightful. And as you learn of this gift, indeed, it can be quite amusing and entertaining and it can bring to you great joy. And you say to me, 'My brethren you speak of entertainment, you speak of, of jolly, you speak of amusement with thot, and manifesting thot.' Most certainly, most certainly, my dear ones. For you cannot manifest your thot with a gloom about it. Is that what you would wish to create? I should hope not. Would you not choose to create, to think that which is beauty, that which is Light, that which brings joy, which causes another to smile, which brings a smile upon your own lips? I say you need not to create with a gloomy thot, or a gloomy frame, for you have much of that upon your plane as it is now.

Know you can create a rainbow? You speak of rainbows, and you put great store within this manifestation. Know you can create one by thinking, thinking, my brethren, thinking. But you must hold the thot. Even the Lord God of Totality held the thot until you came forth as you were to be, and you were given the vessel that you needed. Think of this gift which you have, which you can do by sitting, and appearing to many of your relatives as one napping, or as one deep off in another place. Think what joy is within you, within your thots. Be you the ballerina upon her toes, or the court jester. This is within you for you may think of these. Dwell upon these.

Create with your thots, and be your thots. Manifest all that does come. Great beauty do you have locked within your sleeping vessel. Great love, great joy, great merriment is within you. But you see you have been taught in order to come to the altar of the Everliving God you must come with a downed countenance, and you must crawl upon your knees, and you must speak of your unworthiness. And this has been given to you, rote, after rote after rote. And you recognize if you have enough rote then you don't have to think. See you this? And I am saying take the rote and throw it away. Cut through it, and stand straight and stand tall before the altar of the Everliving God, and say to that which is the Lord God of Totality, 'The Lord God of my being recognizes that I am a manifestation of that which you are. Use of me that I might manifest that which you have sent me to do, that I might grow in myne own totality.' And you say to me, 'My brethren, this is heavy.' And I say to you 'My brethren, tis so.' For if you are as one think you have not the right to stand before the Lord God of Totality and proclaim who you are, then indeed you are not ready to recognize who you are, and you are not ready to manifest that which you are capable of thinking.

I speak to you this hour to say to you, recognize who you are and that which you have within you. Use this glorious gift of yours called thinking, that you might manifest your own divinity, that which you were sent forth as.

Do you recognize that as you learn to manifest your thoughts you have but to desire, and that which you desire is before you? Yes, you would desire of peace and peace would be of a virtue. You would desire of harmony and you would be as one of harmony. You would desire of beauty and you would be bathed in beauty. Tis not this a most wondrous gift, this which you are, and this which you can do? I will say to you when this realization came to me as I walked upon the planes of Earth, it was a most startling realization. And it was as if I had found or discovered a long forgotten secret. And I practiced from one sunrise to the next, to the next to the next.

I practiced until I could manifest that which I thot. I could desire of travel unto another place, and this I did. But my whole being was used in the manifestation of my thots, for it took the ability to cut out all of the superfluous that is around us that keeps us so busy—and of your plane of this day you have many things that keep you busy that are hollow things, for you reap nothing from the activity. You must cut from these and learn to sit in silence with your thot, hold your thot.

Myne brethren that is known to you as Sananda, that was known as Jesus as he walked the Earth, held the perfect thought within his being. And did he not say to you that greater miracles than he did, that you were capable of doing also? Tis so you kno, tis so. Thot, T-H-O-T. Oh yes, I recognize you have, what have you with the spelling of this word, but I give you the word t-h-o-t, thot; t-h-i-n-k, think; b-e, be. As you think and you form the thot, the perfect thot that you are, so shall you be."

Received by Tuieta   **—Theoaphylos**

"Opening Up to Take a Look—Pearls of Wisdom"

"This God was passive, he was timid and shy—and while experiencing the emotion of being timid and shy, he became very closed and hid His Light from others. This is a True Story! Count on it!

That emotion went through the process and became coagulated thought in the sea—and there was formed wondrous little creature who exemplified the emotions of the God. The creature had a wonderful shell—that covered it's entirety, it was home, *home!* And inside the shell was a creature—very soft tissue, delicate—it never grew old for I have never seen one with wrinkles. But it was very soft, and the little creatuere loved it's wonderful castle that it lived in— and really how convenient of this God to be so considerate—

122

PHOTO BY KEVIN LAHEY

PHOTO BY SISTER THEDRA

while this entity was encased within it's own home it didn't have to pick up and move on, it was just there—all of the conveniences that a soft tissued little creature could possibly have.

So it was feeling rather *jolly good*. And the God looked down upon it—and alas thought it was beautiful—what wondrous creativity—it be shy God became a little arrogant, a little smug, because it was beautiful. No other creature could get it's jowls on it and snap it to pieces, He had fixed that—and so His creation would endure.

The little tissue, of the entity got rather bored with it's surroundings and opened up to take a look at what was about—and when it peered out into the emerald aqua blue in came that which is called a speck of dirt and it got right in it's eye! And it slammed it's doors shut. Ever have a cinder fly into your eye?!

Well it sat there, with all the water in the world it still agitated the little creature, ah the misery of it all. And it fell out of the eye and got under it's belly and with all the laughter that this creature felt, it was rather tickled. After all it becomes a little boring, and the creature sat there with no arms mind you, very soft and did not know what to do with this sand that had come in through the front door. And so the little entity sat there being agitated and it wallowed and flopped and rolled, trying to move over and unfortunately you see that which is called grains of sand they are rather round and so wherever the little entity moved, it followed. And so it was everywhere, and the Great God looked upon the entity and lost His composure—and had really rather reposed Himself because he had not thought of this, what to do? *What to do?*

And so once evolution was taking it's toll on the land and on the Gods who were running amuck in their bodies—they had not yet created fast bodies.

This God stayed aloft and was trying to figure out what to do about this poor wretched little creature. And as He was figuring it out other things began to manifest around His little creature, barnacles and the like—and they were all the after thought of what to do about the creature, so they became a manifestation—but it didn't do any good. So as He was continuing, wrapped up in Himself—the little creature said 'uncle,' it gave up.

So it laid on it's sand and it accepted the grain and as it accepted the grain, it noticed that there came a moment that it felt rather good! And as it was feeling rather good it moved over to take a look and it rolled over to the front of him and looked it right in the eye—and here was the most wondrous, wondrous grain of sand—why the very look at it eye to eye was remarkable. It had company, someone had moved in!! And from all appearances they were planning to stay! This is a *true story!*

So the little tissue became very happy with this entity, and began to love it. It was it's company after all. And it began to adore it and the more it adored it and the happier it became the more beautiful the company became, what a stroke of luck! It was soft, sleek, iridescent and pleasing to the eye—and if you wanted to propie-tarry upon, it was ever so comfortable. And when the God figured it out what he could figure out how to get rid of it, He embraced His little creature, became the little creature—and behold He was astounded at the creatures intelligence. It had taken the irritation, it had *accepted it, embraced it,* and turned the irritation in to *pearls.* This is a true story.

Inside every Pearl is an irritation! The name of this grand and glorious entity, first name was clamatis, it evolved into the oyster. The oyster is liken to you, except learned from the beauty of Life that every limitation, every hurt, every pain, every sorrow, every deception, everything that irritates you, if you *embrace* it and *love* it you *own* it, and the irritation becomes the *pearls* of *wisdom.* you have gained the value of the Pearl this day in your time, you Own it! This hour it is worthy to say 'Alas, I have gained the wisdom, I own it, this is my Pearl.' Every irritation that is embraced and loved and transformed, the transfiguration occurs and your Soul is heavy-laden with the treasure of experience.

Know you why I say unto you that noble virtue is not the abstinence of Life but the embracing of it? For one who abstains from life has an empty Soul. One who is emersed in it, dreams the illusions and the adventures and grasps the wisdom—they are called the 'Gods of Noble Virtue'—and unto them and only them is that which is called the King of *Kings,* the *Christ* availed unto. You do not come back *home* empty handed, you go back *home* rich with treasure—

I love you, so be it.''
Channeled by J.Z. Knight   **—Ramtha**

The Pressure, The Testing— The D-I AM-O-N-D, The Brilliance

''Greetings my brother. I Am Monka to reply. And might I say, most certainly. Yes, there are ones that are of the Dark Brotherhood. And there are ones who by their choice, act as they would think not in agreement with Divine Law. However, I might add a thought here, for your consideration. All is of the Creative Principle, the Divine Creator. That which is known to you as the Dark Brotherhood, are ones who have chosen not to willingly follow of the Creative Principle, but rather to use those gifts that have been given to them in direct opposition to Divine Light. But as within all things, these too are governed by Universal Law. For the Dark Brotherhood has specific areas, specific limitations in which they must work. And as within all things if you give this a fair evaluation and consideration you can see where these ones help to hone, to polish, help each individual to develop on their own in their surety in Light. For those that come forth in the evolutionary process have been tested, have been tried, and have been tempted, and they have been wooed by ones of the Dark Brotherhood. And truly, a diamond does not reach its absolute beauty until it has been, it has undergone a great deal of pressure, then it has been polished and it has been honed, and its true brilliance comes forth. I offer this analogy for your consideration. And I trust this has answered your question.''
Received by Tuieta   **—Monka**

''Other Worlds Beyond One's Own Perspective, Beyond One's Own Limited Confines''

''My beloved chelas of the Diamond Heart, there are some who will say We keep harping on the same old message, but We utilize the words this way and that, turning a phrase, making a point, using analogies, hoping to pry loose a mind from the chains and shackles and encrustations of ages past, which thickly engross one in the dense physical world and allow not the free movement of the Soul. Many are beginning to timidly peek out from within their shells, becoming discontent with the confines of such a rigid structure. They begin to move slowly here and there, then quickly withdraw back into the shell when some alarming or conflicting piece of information comes their way and touches a tender spot. Reactive, would you say? Indeed. And many there are who react so violently that they withdraw completely into the security of that shell and venture forth not again for some time. Thus has been repeated the pattern of the ages that when chastised, seek no more and question not. 'Once burnt, twice shy.' But We can counter that with 'nothing ventured, nothing gained.'

So it is that after a time, those shell walls begin their constricting pulsating and again, the timid one ventures forth,

128

perhaps a little wiser for the experience and hopefully after having summoned up enough courage to step out once again, will look and observe much as a window shopper to familiarize with that which is available, yet somewhat protected from direct contact by the window itself. Thus the mind can become familiar with what is in the other worlds beyond one's own perspective, beyond one's own limiting confines and circle of endeavor. This is where books are most valuable.

At last one decides to venture forth leaving the shell behind but always in the recesses of the mind is the knowledge the shell is still there and if what one approaches is 'hostile' there is the safe retreat. But chelas, that shell must eventually be destroyed, for as long as it is there, even though distant and remote, there is an attachment to which you are drawn in time of conflict and confusion. In order for you to free yourself from this pastlife hindrance and constriction you must destroy it. It is as though you having built it, now have outgrown it and it must be discarded. But when moving to a higher level, be cautious and use the wisdom not to once again construct a rigid structure, for as your consciousness expands, so indeed your perceptions of concepts and your perspective can give you a most prejudiced view. The mind free to pursue the Truth discards what was thought to be truth in your primary stages of development. In the secondary stages a broader perspective is given and the primary Truths are expanded upon. But as you develop further and your scope of knowledge increases, you see that much, much which you viewed was a distortion from the perspective at which you were standing at a given time. This does not negate the Truth but it removes the limited personality coloration from it.

You who seek the Truth must continually relinquish what you had previously deemed as Truth. We cite the example of the Flat Earth theory and also the concept of the Earth as the center of the Solar System or even the Universe. These ideas were deemed as Truth and accepted as fact by men until observers raised their minds higher and changed their perspective. Those concepts which in your primary stages you saw as Truth as but an element of Truth, and distorted they are indeed. As your perspective widens you will see more than you could possibly have imagined, and yet within the limited confines of the mind this is still but a fragment of the whole.

As the Soul growth continues and your knowledge increases, and as the Soul-rapport registers in the conscious mind, your perspective of Reality will change vastly. Be not restricted to that which other men teach, but know within your heart and mind that with which the Soul seeks to imbue you, for as you accept that which the Soul offers, relinquishing that which the personality clings to, indeed your awareness grows, preparing you thus for the Cosmic Experience.

There are those who touch into the Cosmic Mind, which is the Great Collective mind, and to this all can look forward as it is part of the Plan for the evolution of man. But only those who are free and have come out of the shell are able to so achieve this. The shell is a most constricting form which must be discarded and *not* replaced with a newer larger model. So it is that each of you in your individual way must pursue this goal and the disintegration of the shell which in your own time and space you have created your limitations. Now in the Soul's good time will they be dissolved when consciously cooperating in the problem—detaching, dissolving, transmuting, questioning old 'truths' and statements of belief, expanding your awareness far, far beyond the present limited capacity. You have the power—the mind within. *Use it.*

With many blessings, urgings, and promptings I send you Blue Flame Power, *Will* Power, to achieve the goal of Cosmic Consciousness.

—I AM El Morya,
Of the Blue Diamond Shining Mind of The Father
bidding you *Adiue!"*
129 *From 'The Voice of Universarius'*

CHAPTER FIVE

GOVERNMENTS

OF THE WORLD

OR

TO GOVERN
WITHIN
THE ETERNAL

I AM

PHOTO BY ZENON MICHALAK

"Cosmic Hierarchy"

"Cosmic hierarchy is order, organization, and balance. Your own world was created with order, organization, and balance. Although much of the natural order has been disturbed by the ignorance of man, there is still much natural order existing.

Would you say there is hierarchy in an ant colony or a bee hive? No. It is not hierarchy. It is order, balance, and organization. Each creation within the colony or hive performs a certain task or role, and no role is more important or vital than another. They are just different, and all are necessary for the good of the Whole. It is organization which is necessary to maintain balance and order. Without it chaos would be present, resulting in the destruction of the Whole.

On the Cosmic level we are all expressions of the Source, performing differing functions in order to maintain order and balance within the Cosmos. The Creator expresses through His creations, thus insuring balance and order and the continuing life in the Cosmos. And like the hive or the ant colony, no position, role, or function is less important than another. All are necessary for the life of the Whole.

Look at your business, governments, and organizations upon your planet. You talk of Hierarchy. It is hierarchy only if you define hierarchy as organization created to establish and maintain order and balance within the framework of the Whole. Without realizing it perhaps, Man has patterned these things after Nature which was patterned after a Cosmic order.

Some entities are disturbed by the idea of hierarchy because they define it as a ladder in which some creations are more important than others and in which some creations are subject to another. This does create a distasteful idea of the Cosmos if you look at it this way.

Looking at it this way you might think that those entities guiding you or communicating to you from other dimensions, and those entities from other sun systems are better than you. We, and they, are not. We are just different, and are expressing the Creator in a different way. You, of Earth, are also expressions of the Creator, and are just as much a part of the Cosmic Whole as we are, and are just as important.

Please remember that 'hierarchy is only organization designed to establish and maintain order and balance.' It has nothing to do with one aspect of creation being better than another. And as creations you are subject to no one or nothing except the Creator, and since you were formed from the Creator, you will, by your very nature, express His nature in varying ways. The natural movement of Creation is always towards order and balance, so even if chaos is present it will always move to restore order and balance."
Channeled by 'Universalia'   —Apollo

What I Really AM
from the Lord Most High

"I AM many things and the human mind is incapable of knowing all, or even understanding, because of their limiting definitions. I AM, first of all, Energy. Everything known is Energy. I AM Movement with Mind. I pour My Mind into all that I have created out of My Energy. I AM fragmented, yet Whole. I have Personality because of the personalities of My expressions. I AM male and female and neither. You love because I Love and you are a part of Me. You give because I Gave and you are a part of Me. You live because I Live and you are a part of Me. I manifest My Thoughts into reality. Yet, what you see as reality is unreal. Only the Essence is real. I AM the Essence of All that is known and unknown to you. I AM Vibration and Movement. I AM Intelligent Energy capable of creating intelligent energy. I have no beginning and I have no end. I know all things in all realms. I AM never away from you for I AM In you and surrounding you. You need never fear Me. Fear comes only when you willfully separate from Me. I AM not an old man sitting in the clouds. Some seem to think of Me and speak to Me as if this were true. I manifested My Expression in the Christ who is My Child just as you are and He tried to teach you where I AM. So many did not listen. I AM totally Connected to All Creation. I AM Power. I AM ever-moving, never still. For Life is Movement. Love is Movement. Allow your mind to escape its finite limits and you will see Me in My Essence. It is done by not limiting your thoughts of Me. I AM beyond man's perception of My Being. I walk in a black man's shoes; I sit upon a king's throne; I die of hunger in India; I travel in the great starships. I AM a flower in the field and the bread upon your table. I AM your table; I AM the field; I AM the star ship; I AM India. Expand your consciousness of yourself and your own potential. I AM trying hard to get willing humans to see beyond their limited vision. I AM; and so, My children, are you. Accept your Sonship as the Christ accepted His. The way you can serve Me best is to *be,* for I AM with you. Don't you understand that we are One and that I will work and walk in you? This is easy if you will but allow it. My Way is easy. My Way is easier than your own ego's. Never be sad for I AM with you and in you and around you.

Channeled by 'Universalia' **—I AM**

"One Day, In The Not Too Distant Future"

"Greetings Tuieta. I am Andromeda Rex speaking to you this morning from the command ship of our Beloved Radiant One.

As you look about you at the sun, and the beauty of summer at the height of its season, it is a time of peace and goodness. Know that it is not so on all parts of your planet. There are those that cry in hunger and have no cover over their heads. This is a direct result of greed and selfishness on the part of the leaders of the world. There is ample food to feed the hungry of the world, but man in his struggle for power uses the very bread of survival to wield his power. Truly this is the epitome of the strength of the forces of darkness, to put one's self above the needs of others.

As others are fed and given sustenance for living, truly do all grow, and the natural laws are observed. The ones that seek to govern, shall not be the self indulgent and egotistical, but the ones that govern within the Law of the Love and the Eternal I AM. One day, in the not too distant future, this will be the rule on Earth, not as it is at this hour.

Our planets and galaxies have learned this, and We are eager to share it with the inhabitants of Earth."

Received by Tuieta **—Andromeda Rex**

"For I Am the Greatest Teacher of All in That"

"In that which is termed as it were, my desire to be here—one because I love you and promised you ere a long time ago, which is only a breath away, that I would come back to you—and I have. Because you have slept a long time. And I know what is cultivating itself here because I gained the wisdom of knowingness a long time ago.

In all the things that I shall do henceforth, will be the rendering of self—for I AM the greatest teacher of all in that, for I have been *you.* No one can tell you how to live unless they've been you. No one."

Channeled by J.Z. Knight **—Ramtha**

"We Know What You Are Experiencing"

"Each of us on our planets has been at that spot within the cycle where you are now. We know what you are experiencing. And at the time that we were experiencing this, others came to assist us. And at this time we most gladly come that we might assist you. For as the cycles go on so shall you one day hold forth your hand to help others. And so it goes. My brother have you gotten the picture that I have given to you?"

Received by Tuieta —**Hatonn**

"Your Governing Powers All Realize That We Exist!"

"We also have our homes and loved ones on our native Planet. Many of us work for long periods of time before the change-over that allows us to return to our home base. Our Mother-Crafts are so large that your three dimensional minds would find them inconceivable. From this base or rather these bases, our smaller craft operate. We monitor your waters and oceans to see just how far your pollution has regressed them and the life that habitates them.

We delve into your great mountains, and within your Earth's crust, but unlike you who are the natural habitants, we do not harm your Planet in any way.

Your governing powers all realize that we exist; they have at many intervals received messages from us. But either will not, or they dare not admit publicly that we exist. So, they secretly investigate us, secretly from you, but not from us, for you should realize from your own television coverage, that nothing is really hidden if you have the eyes to see it, and believe me we have the eyes."

Received by Joan Brown, England

"Ones in High Government Offices Have Heard From Us Directly"

Question: "Why is it that our governments have kept all information concerning space beings from us?"

"I am Hatonn to reply. Your government, as well as most governments of Earth, is a state or is in a state of egomania. Each strives to convince its people that they are the superior force within a specific area. I would ask you for a moment to gaze upon your country and those that lead your country. This is a mighty nation, this nation of your United States of America. It was founded on principles that were Divinely brought forth. And these were written by the hand of Masters embodied on your Earth. Great ones volunteered to come forth to serve during your country's inception. And since the day that your country has declared its independence and has stood for the rights of free men, that it has stood for the ideals of brotherhood and of the Great White Brotherhood, this has been a country that has been respected. For those of other countries about your Earth that have been put down, that have been down-trodden, they have looked to this country, to ones of this country with admiration and respect. Thus, this has been the state that your country has earned.

Now unfortunately, as your country has progressed from its ideal state, the idea of being the greatest, the most perfect and the most powerful has stayed with ones of government. Now, would you be the greatest and the biggest and the most perfect and the most powerful if you acknowledge there was a force outside this Earth that could communicate with you? A force you have not seen. A force that has vehicles, has ships, that cannot be touched by your bullets, by your warheads. Ones, that when you draw near in a hostile manner, they merely disappear. Would this make you feel superior and comfortable if you acknowledged this to the peoples that you govern? Unfortunately the approach has been, no: 'So we *shall be silent upon all of this. We shall not acknowledge a presence external to Earth. We shall acknowledge no superior force except our own.'*

Though I assure you, ones in high government offices have heard from us directly. And there has been a very specific communication with your country and with other predetermined countries within your world.

And now I must apologize for it would seem that I have rambled and this was not my intent, but I do hope this has answered your question."
Received by Tuieta **—Hatonn**

regardless! They, in their ignorance of Spiritual Laws, do not realize the full significance of what is happening at the present time—nor will they do so, until the Moment is upon them. So we bide our time, as you bide yours—knowing how the end must be. Therefore, we are not disheartened . . . ."

" 'By their fruits you shall know them' . . . it has been said many times, and it is as true today as it was two thousand years ago, or will be two thousand years hence, 'By their fruits ye shall know them.' "

—We Wish You Goodnight

"Govern(mental) Predicaments"

"You see, the predicament of most of your governments throughout the world, necessitates their trying to cope with a crumbling system, a situation of chaos and disintegration of the status quo; if they were to release the information they hold, it would add to the chaos and confusion—and to some extent, the lawlessness, which already abounds. For when men and women realize that they have been 'hood-winked,' as you would say, for so many years, —that the truth has been withheld from them by men in power, that Earth-people are relatively unevolved, that there *are* Celestial Chariots and Celestial Scripts—that the Churches have failed to give them the Truth as to the sublime Nature of Existence and the Creator's Eternal Love, Mercy and Justice—if the peoples of the Earth became aware of the deliberate suppressions and procrastinations of their leaders they would tear them apart in their frenzied rebellion.

They stave-off the day when they shall be pulled down from power—this is *the reason for the secrecy!*—to maintain the status quo is to maintain their positions of power—

"Much to the Dismay of Government Officials"

"That those of governmental rule are not there to enlighten the people but to keep them under that which is termed the 'thumb' to shelter. Their context, master, has been very shrewd, very clever and very good to the common peoples.

It is through the common belief of all the people who make up the composite of the land, master, that *they* (the Guardians) will make their ultimate presentation to—much to the dismay of government officials I assure you."

—Ramtha

Question: "So you are saying that Government officials are not feigning ignorance when they say they believe there is little to the UFO phenomenon?!"

"Ignorance as it were indeed—it is contrary to their belief, master, **they believe in them to be sure,** and are perplexed that they are not a participant in that which is termed the phenomenon—they believe in them it is true."
Channeled by J.Z. Knight **—Ramtha**

142

PHOTO DONATED BY W. & J EVERETT
TAKEN IN BAJA, CALIFORNIA

PHOTO BY KEVIN LAHEY

"Ones of Your Astronauts That Have Seen Our Ships"

Question: "Could you tell us about your feelings of the space ships that we send up? Do you see them, and do you know if they (our astronauts) see you?"

"We see the ships that are sent up. We see the satellites that are circling. And in many instances we have had to alter, or rather shall I say modify, some of the flight patterns of some of the ones that have come forth from your Earth. There have been ones of your astronauts that have seen our ships, that have seen evidences of our landings upon your moon. Though, your government does not choose to share this information with you at this time. It is hoped that in future days they will share this. Yes, they have seen us, and we have seen them. And I must say your ships do lack in convenience . . . "

Received by Tuieta   **—Monka**

"I Say That There Were Other Space Ships"

"During the transmission of the moon landing of Armstrong and Aldrin who journeyed to the moon in an American spaceship, two minutes of silence occurred in which the image and sound were interrupted. NASA insisted that this problem was the result of one of the television cameras which had overheated thus interfering with the reception. This unexpected problem surprised even the most qualified of viewers who were unable to explain how in such a costly project, one of the most essential elements could break down, an element which was to serve to convince the world of the level of technology which had been achieved by the United States. Some time after the historic moon landing, Christopher Kraft, director of the base in Houston, made some surprising comments when he left NASA.

The contents of these comments which is included in the conversations, which here has been corroborated by hundreds of amateur radio operators who had connected their stations to the same frequency through which the astronauts transmitted. During the two minute interruption—which was not as it seemed, NASA, Armstrong and Aldrin with Cape Kennedy, censored both image and sound. *"I say that there were other spaceships."*

Here is reproduced completely the dialogue between the American astronauts and Control Center:

Armstrong & Aldrin: "Those are giant things, No, no, no—this is not an optical illusion. No one is going to believe this !"

Houston: "What . . . what . . . what? What the hell is happening? What's wrong with you?"

Armstrong & Aldrin: "They're here under the surface."

Houston: "What's there (muffled noise) Emission interrupted; interference control calling 'Apollo II.' "

Armstrong & Aldrin: "We saw some visitors. They were there for a while, observing the instruments."

Houston: "Repeat your last information!"

Armstrong & Aldrin: "I say that there were other spaceships. They're lined up in the other side of the crater."

Houston: "Repeat, repeat!"

Armstrong & Aldrin: "Let us sound this orbita . . . In 625 to 5 . . . Automatic relay connected . . . My hands are shaking so badly I can't do anything. Film it? God, if these damned cameras have picked up anything—what then?"

Houston: "Have you picked up anything?"

Armstrong & Aldrin: "I didn't have any film at hand. Three shots of the saucers or whatever they were that were ruining the film."

Houston: "Control, control here. Are you on your way?

What is the uproar with the UFO's over?"

Armstrong & Aldrin: "They've landed there. There they are and they're watching us."

Houston: "The mirrors, the mirrors—have you set them up?"

Armstrong & Aldrin: "Yes, they're in the right place. But whoever made those spaceships surely can come tomorrow and remove them. Over and out."

"Christopher Kraft, chief of the Houston base, commented: 'The reaction of our men has been very unusual, but I don't doubt that space has influenced them in everything. The example of Armstrong's modesty is not without impact, and Aldrin's altruism provides food for thought. In any case, I think that they all had something in common as they came back to earth better men than when they left it."

"They Shall Be Accepted"

"They (The Guardians) will make their advent to a few, and the few as it were indeed, will multiply and become more and more and they shall be accepted."
Channeled by J.Z. Knight   **—Ramtha**

"The Moon Shot"

The Archangel Gabriel speaks on "The Moon Shot"—April 26, 1962, 7:30 a.m.: "Beloved: When it is come that they learn that they are within the Earth bound they will be as ones prepared for a new part—I say they shall be as ones which have within their hand the power to destroy themselves—and they shall be as ones tormented of their own willfulness and wanton (rebelliousness). I say they shall abide by the law—or be the victims of that which they have set into motion.

I am only a spectator in 'this affair' of man; I am sent to guard my own—I am not prepared to deliver up the wanton, for it is with their own free will that they do that which they do, and I am not permitted by law (that is, the Law of the universe in which ye are at present—and I am not of a mind to betray my self nor my trust). I am not permitted to interfere with their free will unless they go so far that the planet be thrown out of her orbit prematurely and aborted.

I am in no way responsible for them as individuals—but I am responsible for the Earth and the course of the Earth—and for the wanton of them which set themselves up in high places—they are responsible unto the Father, and the Father has entrusted unto me this part, and woe unto any man which sets his hand against me.

I say I am not of a mind to forfeit my inheritance: it has been done by one which was *'a Son of God'* and they which followed him are yet paying the price!

I say he was the *'Son of God'* once in time gone—but he too thought himself *The Most High,* and was cast down—and he is now the 'Prince of Perdition'—and so shall it be until he has paid unto the last jot and tittle. I say he shall pay unto the last farthing! I am one known as the *Porter* (guardian) of thy world."   **—I AM Gabriel of the Star Ship**
Recorded by Sister Thedra

(The previous message was recorded simultaneously with the news of the U.S.A. "Moon Shot")

148

"The Fall of A Son of God"

"Was it not said that there was a war in heaven? And was it not so? For it was given unto one which was a Son of God to betray himself—For he had the power invested within him of God the Father to create even worlds—yea to create and to populate them—and he has within his power even to this day to create them. Yet I say unto thee my daughter Thedra that when he gave unto himself and when he took unto himself the glory he became as one puffed up—as one rebellious—and he gathered about him the ones which were of like mind and they gave unto him great glory and they were fascinated by his words—and by his miracles—and he gave unto them words of praise and appointed unto them grand places and stations and called them by great sounding names and brought royal raiment and placed it upon them with great high courts attending."

Recorded by Sister Thedra   **—Mother Sarah**

"She Is To Be Elevated To Her Reward"

"We have heightened the frequency of the energies poured forth in order to help to stay Mother Earth in her present orbit and on her present course. We continually monitor all of you and all of mankind on Earth to note any change in the frequencies of each one. It has been noted most recently that there are those within high places of governments upon your planet, that are endeavoring to bring about what they would call world supremacy. Unfortunately, their definition of supremacy is annihilation for all of Earth. I will assure now, and in the future, *this will not be.* We shall intercede most directly in the event that such action is taken. Be assured dear ones, Mother Earth shall not be denied her place in the Total Plan. Indeed, she shall not be denied her place within this universe, for there is need of her, her energies, and it is to be that she is to be elevated to her reward

for all of her struggles. However, our activity at this time is to deal with these ones that are most eager to prove their point. Alas, they show a great immaturity and unworthiness for the positions they hold. Though they sit in councils as representatives of the peoples of their countries and as heads of governments, they truly are not deserving of these roles, for they seek only to glorify and exalt the 'I' within themselves. For these ones I weep, for they have not learned their lessons, though many times they have walked about the Earth.

But to you dear I would say, walk each day in Light, project Light and Love to all, be the Light you are capable of being. Be the vessel to be filled with the Love of the Divine One. As this you truly do, then naught but Love and Light shall come to you. You shall be ones that are prepared regardless of what transpires about you. You shall be ones that shall be anchored. This is your particular assignment. This is your role. Be Light. Be Love. Maintain your balance and harmony. Be at one with Creation and Creative Force.

Blessings I send each of you. My love I abundantly share with each of you, I am your brother, a humble servant of the Most High."

Received by Tuieta   **—I AM Kuthumi**

"That No Harmful Unbalance Was Sent Forth Throughout The Universe"

"As you are aware by the note of frivolity within my speech, we are in a state of preparation and we are in a state of readiness. We merely are on stand-by at this hour awaiting the decision of man and that he would do. I might with your indulgence comment on the missile that was sent forth on this your calendar day. And I might also comment on its effect. Yes, this missile reached its target. But I assure you, before it reached its target it was deactivated so that no harmful unbalance was sent forth throughout the universe. Within this missile there was sufficient nuclear energies and bombardments that could have caused quite a disturbing imbalance within your earthly plane. We of the Fleet concentrated great energy upon this as it was dispatched into our area of existence that it was neutralized, that no untoward effects were felt throughout this universe or the Cosmos. We recognize the thought behind sending forth such a missile at this time, though it truly was an inopportune act. It was not necessary. **It was not necessary.**

There were ones on your plane that petitioned most earnestly that this act not be manifested. These ones had our thoughts, our prayers that they shared. And we were in close communion in an attempt to help sway the decision makers of your government. Again, I shall repeat, supremacy one country over the other is not your answer for a lasting peace for Mother Earth. Might I suggest, or I would suggest that you, each one of you, use the opportunities that are available to work toward universal peace, to work for the cessation of atomic weapons and such. These are not your answer. This is not your way.

There is little left for us to do as far as our preparatory phase is concerned. We of the Fleet are on stand-by awaiting the actions of mortal man, awaiting the cycle of events to follow one upon the other."

Received by Tuieta   **—Hatonn**

"Intervention of a Drastic Nature"

"We warn your leaders, with much love and concern, that intervention of a drastic nature will take place in your midst if you persist to a conclusion, your preparations to plunge the planet Earth into full-scale nuclear conflagration. Under existing Universal Law and Intergalactic Allied Agreement, *you will not be permitted to do this.* The decision is in your hands, to a certain point. Should you determine to pursue your present course, you will *no longer remain in control of your planet.* Both intervention and invasion will be initiated which will preserve the Earth and its surrounding galaxy.

It is now time for humanity to cease from its childish war games and become *man,* with an awakened sense of his responsibility and accountability for life on Earth. In spite of the many now on Earth who plot and plan otherwise, this planet will yet become a member of its own peaceful solar system and galaxy, and will become a part of the Universal Alliance for Peace."

Received by Tuella   **—Ashtar**

" 'A New Generation'—They Shall Go To War No More"

"Beloved Ones:—This day let it be understood that service unto one's country is not enough, it is not sufficient unto thine salvation.

For to love one another is without counterpart, it is the greatest of all 'Service'—service unto thine brother men, men of thine own, which are like unto thee—these are thine own kind—yet there is *more;* Consider well: Who is thine brother? Wherein is the other excluded, for reason that he has his habitat in a foreign land? Or that he wears a garment of another color? I say unto thee: 'Love ye one another, and thou shall *not kill!*'

While it is now come that they shall raise up against an unjust system, and great persecution—I say unto the oppressed, and the down trodden: 'A new generation shall be raised up, which shall go to war no more, they shall bring about a *new order,* a *new system!* and war shall be outlawed.' So be it according unto the *will* of Mine Father which hast sent *me.*

PHOTO BY KEVIN LAHEY

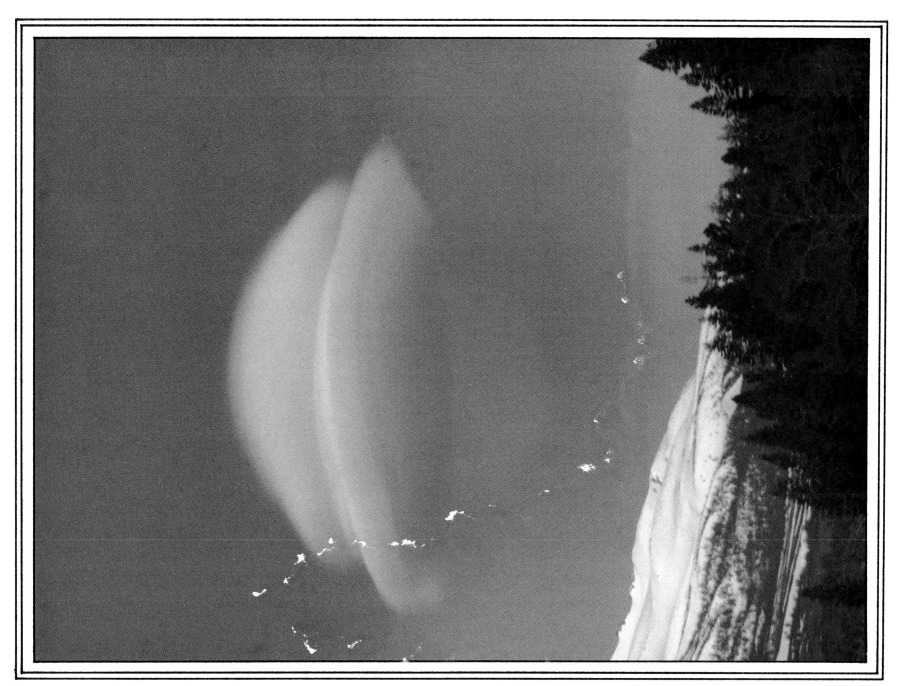

PHOTO BY MICHAEL RADFORD

I speak out this day, as One Sent, that there be Light in the world of men—I say a *new generation* shall be raised up, and they shall *no more go to war!* So be it I have spoken, and I shall speak again and again.

I shall raise Mine Voice against the oppressors, and the ones which sit in high places, and think themselves wise!"

—So be it I AM the Lord thy God, **San Anda**
Recorded by Sister Thedra

"A New Garden of Julian"

"And there shall be a new people, and they shall know that which is of the Father. And there shall be a new Garden of Julian, and therein shall be the Father's *kingdom* upon the Earth. And it shall be for the good of all that there shall be one who shall reign supreme, yet they shall work as one man.

And there shall be peace. And each man shall be peace unto himself, and he shall be as the keeper of the peace. And he shall be as the lawgiver and the keeper thereof, for he shall know that which is ethical and he shall abide thereby. And there shall be none among them which shall covet another's possessions, nor shall they know hatred.

For it is established that the new Kingdom shall be established upon the Lotus which now lies within the bed of the Pacific Ocean.

And it shall be that there shall be peace and harmony, and it shall reign for the cycle which shall last for twelve thousand years. And again she shall be in a new cycle which shall bring another order—and therein is another story . . .

And for the time being we are interested only with the next decade which shall bring about many unbelievable changes, and they shall be as tragedy at the time; yet considering that which is eternal—has no beginning nor end—what is there to fear? And why is there anything of thy apportioned lot that ye shall fear?

☆ ☆ ☆

And she shall shine in all her glory; and she shall be peopled with the ones which have awakened and those which shall remember that which has been. And they shall know that which shall be, for they shall be one with the Father. And they shall know that which is of the Father and that which is of the Earth.

And therein shall they abide within the law which is of the Eternal Verities. And they shall not be bowed down with the pity of the Earth as it is now upon the Earth, for it is indeed a pity to see them which stirreth not; they walk with eyes which see not, and they are deaf unto the call of the Clarions, which have been sent unto them for their own sake.

And within the time which is near they shall see and they shall hear, and they shall be as one which knows not what he sees; yet he shall call out for learning, and it shall not be denied him. For many are among them for the purpose of bringing the light, and it shall not be denied them, nor shall it be forced upon them, for it is unethical for them that would be so foolish.

And within the time which is come they may be as the children of the Father, yet they have forgotten the way unto the Father's house. And they shall cry for help, and it shall be given to them freely and without price.

☆ ☆ ☆

And for the First time, it is told them, that which shall be. And they have not heard the Clarion call, nor have they heard the trumpets which shall sound; and it shall not be symbolic but as literally true as the "bells of St. Marys," for they shall sound."

Recorded by Sister Thedra　　　　　　　　　—**Sananda**

"Little Do They Realize"

"You stand at the threshold of a new major growth cycle, when the Water Bearer (Aquarius) becomes the sign of *spiritual man,* no longer bound by the fetters of earthly dimension, but free to roam the dimensions and worlds at will. This is part of the upcoming soul's purpose for the Planet Earth which must not be destroyed! There are those upon your planet who will do everything within their power to destroy this possibility now, in order to hold man captive to the third dimension. Little do they realize that their plan simply cannot and will not work! The growth of the planet and the humans upon it who are part of its evolutionary cycle must and will be given a chance to proceed with that evolutionary growth process. However, it is the current desperate struggle between Light and Darkness which has us ever watchful. This is the Armageddon.

What can you do to protect yourself? Remain always within the aura of your Father/Mother God. Make His Ways, your ways. Rejoice in the Light and make it your own. Keep that Light around you at all times, and several times a day make the call to your God Self to strengthen and re-enforce that Light shield around you. This is a *must!* According to the amount of Light you can project around yourself, will be the amount of protection accorded by you. Those who consciously walk in the Way of the Father will be protected at all costs. We bless you for reading this message."

—I AM he who is **Joshua,**
Received by Lucy Colson   & I AM he who is **Andromeda Rex**

"Your Time Shortens"

"The leaders of your planet must come together in peace and brotherhood for all of the planet. The present approach your countries are taking with one another is most devastating and will lead to eventual annihilation if you are allowed to continue on your present approach. Fortunately for all souls involved with Earth, the Councils and Confederation will not let your leaders continue to do that. My message is to *all* of Earth, *lay down your weapons, lay down your arms, defuse your bombs, and silence your satellites.* This is the only approach that will have lasting positive consequences. Your conscious implementation of these steps will save you from an irrevocable path of destruction. Eartheans, hear my words. I, Cuptan Fetogia, have seen ones similar to you, destroy their cosmic base. These ones have suffered untold scarring and sorrow. Do not make the same mistake in trying to duplicate what has been done. Your time shortens. Your time shortens! Do not allow your leaders, your ones in positions of responsibility to act in an emotional frenzy."
Received by Tuieta   —**Cuptan Fetogia**

"Frozen Equilibrium"

"Greetings, thou being of Shan*. In the light of love and peace I come to you. Commandant of the station Schare. I am Ashtar. Having returned to the station Schare from the center, I advance to your scientists the following information.

We have told you that the element hydrogen is a living substance. In the composition of your physical being, in the air you breathe, in the water you drink, are five elements of living substance besides hydrogen—the elements nitrogen, oxygen, carbon, fluorine and sodium. Much of your material science has been directed to disproving theory that does not conform to the personal beliefs of some scientific authority. Among the

156

scientific mentalities of this planet, Shan, are many minor scientists, who do not have the authority to change these opinions that have been disproved. We have advanced you information in the faint hope that some of your governmental authorities would grasp the fact, that with the explosion of living substance they create a condition parallel to what your scientists call 'frozen equilibrium.' This release of free hydrogen into the atmosphere of this planet will cause flames to engulf many portions of this planet momentarily.

Those in authority in the governments are assuming direct responsiblity not only for the people inhabiting this planet, but their own immediate families, wives, children, parents and relatives are also their responsibility, for these dear ones shall not escape. You in authority of the governments of the planet Shan, think twice if you would have your loved ones with you. Consult your physicists. Ask them about the parallel condition of frozen equilibrium. They will inform you, if they speak the truth and are not influenced otherwise by the forces of darkness, that this is truth.

Wake up, you who would believe only those who direct you. Stand before the people. Tell those who influence your mental decisions that they, too, are involved. In the light of Love, I transmit you a continuous beam here, through a ventla which has been stationed in this cone of receptivity at a level 72,000 miles above you, beyond reach of any traps. I shall return."

Received by George Van Tassel   —My love, I AM **Ashtar**
(* Shan=Earth)

Note: Speaking with an understanding of forever, our Guardians speak of 'The New Day, The Final Hour, and Momentarily' from their point of vision.

"This Shortens the Cycle"

"I am Monka to reply to your question concerning speed by which your clock moves. You of Earth are involved in several cycles. A cycle here might be defined as a chain of events, as a chain of circumstances where one step follows the next to achieve the next. If the choice is to try to skip part of the steps then the time in earthly terms is shortened. I shall use here briefly an example. Your scientists on Earth have developed the ability to split the atom. They have not been content with those atomic structures that are not living structures. But they have turned to your living elements, consequently, your hydrogen bomb. The living elements are elements that are felt, that are utilized throughout the universe. Thus, there is a chain or a molecular reaction continually between and among all molecules, all atoms involving hydrogen. When this atom is split and there is an explosion upon your earth involving the hydrogen atom, this is felt throughout the universe. Indeed in such an instance it is as if the universe contracts and shudders in the horror of the activity. This shortens the cycle, for it burns up and destroys that which is living and is not to be touched. I trust this has answered your question in some small way."

Received by Tuieta   **—Monka**

"The Law of the 'One' Which Governs All Things"

"Now say I unto 'them' that it is come when a great army of light workers or 'workers in the light' shall go out from the temple of light and they shall be well prepared for that which shall be given unto them to do, for it is now come when many from three different planets have come into the earth that she may be spared that which they have fortuned unto themselves—for they know not that they stand on the brink of destruction.

And they have given themselves credit for being wise. So be it that they shall be confronted with their foolishness, and they shall stand as ones shorn of all their self-gained glory, and of all their so-called scientific knowledge, for it shall avail them naught. And now I say unto thee that they (the workers of light) shall have no weapons other than those of light, love and wisdom, for it is the only weapon which they shall know; and they shall be well prepared to use these, for they shall be prepared as ones who have been trained in the laws of the losoloes and they shall know the law of the 'one' which governs all things. And they shall have the power which shall be invested within them of the Father; they shall have the authority which He shall will unto them; and they shall have the wisdom to command the law and it shall obey their command, so be it and Selah.

Now ye shall stand in the place of the Most High Living God and receive from the Father's own hands the fortune which he has willed unto thee. So be it and Selah. Now ye shall say unto 'them' as I would say, that they shall be as small children which have found their way into the place wherein is kept the firearms of war (arsenal) which know not the plan or the power with which they are playing.

That is given in simple words which they cannot misunderstand, so be it that they cannot say 'they do not understand my words'—it is the law which they do not understand!

So be it that they shall come to know the folly of their mad rush to get into 'space'—to get into the firmaments; to reach out for a foothold—and so be it, they shall not be perminted a foothold for greed and conquest! So be it, they shall cry out as ones in despair! for they shall come into the age of accountability before they destroy themselves and the earth which has given unto them a place of abode! Now ye shall give unto them these words, and it shall profit them to hear and heed them, for I am not of a mind to stand still while they destroy themselves: So be it that I shall send out them which have the power and authority to bring them in! Now ye shall turn a deaf ear if ye will—but I am sent that ye may hear me, and I shall not be denied! And ye shall be made to hear; so be it, ye shall come to know me, for I shall set up my banner and nothing shall prevail against it! I am a man of 'Peace' yet my wrath shall know no bounds! for I am come to make way for peace and I shall not be outdone. So be it, I am sent of the Father that His will may be done on the earth, so be it and Selah."

Recorded by Sister Thedra   **—I AM Sananda**

"The Intergalactic Pact"

"Greetings and blessings in the Light of the Divine Creator. I am Monka speaking. It is that the hour has come to give to you that which you thought was lost. Not so dear sister, not so. Nothing is ever lost. This you must grasp. It is merely beyond your grasp at a specific interlude. Do not be over emotional at that which was done. Receive the lesson that was given and know you have grown in the lesson. One lesson that has so far eluded you is that you are not of the super human portion and you cannot expect yourself to be that. There must be a time when you say to others to stop. You must have time to recharge and rebalance. You were out of balance and that is the reason of your forgetfulness. As you scan your past experiences the times that you have committed the errors have been when you were out of balance because of fatigue. Is there not a lesson in this? The lesson is there for all as well as for yourself. Blessings to you and to all who partake of these words.

But now to continue. The question was put forth con-

PHOTO BY MICHAEL RADFORD

cerning the reason for our involvement with you of Earth. Long before your recorded history there was a planet in this universe that was most beautiful. It would easily be described as your Garden of Eden. The beings there had the opportunity to be quite evolved. They were evolved to the point that they literally blew-up their beautiful planet. The reverberations were felt throughout the Cosmos. Not only was this universe shaken, but all of the others as well. This act of selfishness was felt in great waves throughout the Cosmos. A great unbalance was experienced as all ones began to put together that which had been rocked by the explosion of the planet.

It was a mourning time for those that were of the other planets and stars of this universe. It was a time that was used as one of great reflection and contemplation. All ones, leaders from all the inhabited planets and stars throughout the Cosmos gathered together to discuss what could be done. They knew within their hearts that this type of act should not be committed again. So the Intergalactic Pact was drafted. In this pact, we stated that in the event that ones, of one of the planets and stars, should ever evolve to the point of being able to destroy a portion of that which had been created, we would, with Divine Permission, be able to enter to terminate their efforts. We would be able to use the Cosmic Laws to alter their planned course of action. The evolution of that particular planet would not be terminated by the selfish actions of the few. But by Divine Law and by the agreed actions of all ones of the Intergalactic Pact, there would be no intercession into the evolutional progression of those ones on that planet, to alter the course of individual choice, if that choice was not detrimental to the total of the populous. So was the pact drawn and signed as it were, to use your terms of Earth.

It is now in this last fifty years that you of Earth have the ability to blow up your planet. You have the ability to try to alter the course of choice for others that have not willingly surrendered up this to you. It shall not be done. By the Intergalactic Pact it shall not be done. So it is that we monitor your actions, that in the event that one of you of Earth take upon your shoulders the act of explosion, we will immediately intercede. Each of you must be given the opportunity to play out your individual drama, to remove yourselves from that which is known to you as the karmic wheel.

In addition to the above given, Mother Earth has volunteered to take upon her shoulders the students of the universes. She has accepted the ones that were of the planet that was destroyed. She has accepted the ones that were slow in their evolution in other areas, to allow them the opportunity to evolve more to their own rhythm. Long ago she has accepted these. So recognize that many of these ones are indeed relatives of ones that are involved in the Intergalactic Pact. These are the brothers and sisters that have chosen a more leisurely route of progression. It is that all things, all ones have of their time. The time, as you would say of Mother Earth, is come that she would go into her new cycle of evolution, she would assume a new berth. So it is that she shall, through the evolutional process, take upon herself the 'progems' or the unresolved energies of much of this universe. The portion of the cycles is such that these unresolved energies shall be lifted from her and from all ones that are to be with her in the next berth. There is a natural progresssion and order to all things—please remember this. Another one will take on those that have not graduated to be with Earth. But please remember that even this one and the ones that will go with her will be at a higher vibrational and evolutionary height than they had been when they entered the cycle for Earth.

Now I have mentioned the cycles. There are three major cycles that are closing at that point that you would call your close of the century, your year 2,000. There are several lesser cycles that are also closing, but for the most part let us be concerned with the three major ones. Earth is to rotate into its new berth. It is to have the opportunity to cast from it all the unresolved energies that have floated with it through the cycles. It is to enjoy the period where it is of balance and harmony. And all ones with it shall be of the same vibrational frequency. Here I will add one thought. Man on Earth has sped up his cosmic clock, for the year 2,000 is much closer than you realize.

In order to assist you of Earth, we of the Council have come to help you to let Earth remain in its present berth to allow as much opportunity as possible for ones on this plane to realize a balance in their evolvement. Please notice that I have not used the word karma, for to be of the karma that has been associated with Earth is to be out of balance with the creative force and Divine Principle. We recognize that there are many that would have been absorbed into the Absolute if it had not been for Earth to give them the opportunity to evolve, just as this new school house shall do. We have come both in the seen and the unseen manifestation to assist in the stabilization of Earth, and ones of Earth, until the hour when Earth shall move into her new berth. She shall go through the birthing process as you have been given, for she shall give up that which is not of her vibrational frequency to take on that which is. As she has the opportunity to evolve so do all ones of this solar system.

We of the other planets and stars recognize what is happening. Most ones on Earth do not. We are involved to allow as much enlightenment as possible for ones of Earth to enable them to enter into the same frequency that Mother Earth will assume as she is lightened. We come in peace and universal brotherhood. We come both in physical manifestation, and in that dimension that is not easily observable by you, to assist. We come to share that which we have received.

We come to encourage those volunteers that have entered Earth at this hour. We come to express the universal hope that there is *light,* there is the at-one-ment that has been so elusive to you up to this hour.

So ones do ask, what is our reason for involving ourselves with you of Earth. My reply is that we love you. We are of the same seed that was sent forth at the beginning. We recognize of the Divine Purpose of all things. We are one with you. Why should we be involved? Why indeed???"

Received by Tuieta   **—Monka**

CHAPTER SIX

CHANGE, PREPARATION,

SURVIVAL

AND

VICTORY

"Greet the New Day and Fear Not"

"Beloved Ones: Let this day bring unto thee fulfillment of *all* the *scripts*—*all* the Holy *Word,* for I say unto thee, this is the day of fulfillment; this is the "End times"—the time of the end, when it shall be finished and done; to be repeated no more! So let it Be as the Father hast willed it.

Hasten yet to meet this day with gladness; greet the *new* day and fear not! For it is now come when ye shall have great assistance. For this have *we* the *'Mighty Host'* revealed ourself unto thee."

Recorded by Sister Thedra   **—I AM Sananda**

"Cleansing and Remodeling"

"Earth—as a playground and educational institution—is *closing down for a period.* After a cleansing and remodeling has transpired, it will be reopened, but with a greater curriculum and staff to challenge the eager students of life into more preparations for even greater horizons that will challenge them after graduation. After successful preparations, those returning to Earth will know the laws and be prepared to live in harmony with them."

"Purification of the Planet"

"Sori Sori—Mighty is He who has come to bring the Word from the Father and to awaken His sleeping brothers in Earth. For too long have they slept, and their awakening will come as a shock to the core of their being. Prepare for the great changes that even now are upon and within the places of Earth. Although it has been described through many sources, man cannot conceive of the completeness of the changes attendant to the purification of thy planet and that which surrounds her.

As with any new birth, pain and suffering will accompany her for a time, but then soon be forgotten in the joy of the new life which she will bring forth. So be it and Selah."

Recorded by Sister Thedra

"As She Moves Out Into Another Berth"

"And think not that the earth is alone, for as she moves out into another berth so shall the other planets of the solar system move, and they are as one and shall move as one in harmony. Ye have not conceived of the vastness of the universe, of the omniverse!"

Recorded by Sister Thedra   **—Sonic**

Note: Sonic is one of the Twenty-four Elders. His gift to us is that of song.

"The New Foundation"

"You are all moving into a higher dimension and you must 'gear' your thoughts and actions to it. That which has been your 'ceiling' will now become your floor, 'the new foundation beneath you.' But any effort expended to attain it you will look back and say, 'Yes, it was well worth it.' "

—Your Mentor from Liason Command Headquarters, **Alon**

Recorded by KaRene

"From Plane Unto Plane And From Dimension Unto Dimension"

"For the great tide of Love and Forgiveness sweeps over this planet today, giving understanding to troubled ones, and Peace unto those who work out in the storms and the winds of change. As this time of Change continues, it is well for the Children of Light to be affirmative of their own protective energies of safety in the Light.

The surety of Faith, and the achievements in the Light, give unto the Children of Light the Knowledge that all is well, no matter what storms may rage on the lower levels of the planet. There is no greater area of positive protection than the knowing that all is well, and that life is yours, no matter in what dimension of achievement. For there is great blessing in work done for the sense of learning and achievement, in the gathering of precious Wisdom, and the ability to work successfully and well with Divine Energies. For those things which seem to be of Good and Light and Love on this plane of understanding, are only the manifestation of the Rays of Love and Wisdom, from the Great expressions of the Rays of Love and Wisdom of the Source of all things, which express in glorious Light, from the plane unto plane and from dimension unto dimension. In this world they shine through the channels of Light, or the Children of One, who express in these densities on these planes of lesser understanding, the Glories of the Great Source of All Light."

Received by Sarah Gran   **—I AM Kwan Yin**

"The Heavens Yet Un-Explored"

"Let it be given unto them as I give it unto thee; and it shall suffice them that *I AM* the *One Sent* that they be lifted up. For this I come, and for this am I here. *I AM* the Lord of Lords, The Host of Hosts, and I say unto thee this day: It is now come when Great and Glorious *Work* shall be accomplished; and Great shall be the Glory of the *New Day*. I say: 'Great shall be the Glory of the New Day' for it shall bring forth *Great Light,* and *Marvels* such as man hast not known; and man shall no longer be bound by the attraction of the Moon, for it shall hold no attraction for him. He shall break his own bounds, and he shall arise as the Phoenix, and swift shall be his ascent; I say: 'Swift shall be his ascent'; and he shall be swift as the arrow in its flight, and sure his mark; for I say he shall *know* whither he goest, and it shall profit him. Let it be known that the doors shall swing wide before him; yet he shall be as one prepared to enter in. It shall be for the good of *all* that he pass within the boundaries of the Heavens yet un-explored.

Now I say: It is come when the doors stand ajar, and man of Earth shall pass—when he hast so prepared himself. Yet there is a time and a way; and it shall come to pass that he shall be as the porter—he shall find his way, and none shall say him 'nay,' for when he hast so prepared himself, he shall arise as on wings, and he shall make his ascent as the Mighty Falcon; he shall be independent of all 'gadgets,' all clumsy machinery. He shall go out as one swift in flight—unafraid and with dignity; I say: With dignity he shall go out unafraid, as one prepared."

Recorded by Sister Thedra   **—Sananda**

PHOTO BY SISTER THEDRA

PHOTO BY KEVIN LAHEY

PHOTO BY KEVIN LAHEY

"The New Kingdom That Is Being Born of Light"

"Man is still playing games. He has not yet awakened to his true destiny or divinity. He thinks only of what he is to become in a material sense. Nor does he link that which encompasses his being and his life as a part of his thinking. Nay! He calls it his 'tough luck' if things go not as he wishes.

He does not realize that by his own vision he can change the pattern of his life. Ah! . . . he feels it is much easier to blame someone else for his downfall. But himself . . . *never!*

Oh Man! To what low rung of the ladder has thou descended unto? Look up and reach that which is above; for only then can the heavens change and that which is of the earth will rise to meet the heavenly force also.

But Man is not using all the tools that are now allotted him. He only looks to his *now* needs. He does not project into the future and look in all directions.

Few there be who look up into the skies of heaven and see the new Kingdom that is being born of Light. It is up there, lying in wait for Man to bring its vision down to Earth. Ah, but can this be done? It is not that Man will have to rise heavenward and become a Being of Light himself, before being accepted in the New Era, the New World that is to come? Man must reach up to that *higher level* of himself, he cannot expect the New World to come down to his level!

Then you will ride no more, Man, in the ancient carts of long Ago; but ride with the *wings of heaven* across the New Horizon and become as a giant of Wisdom, learning of naught but the Wisdom of the New Age. For the Fabric of Time has wrought miracles in releasing to the New Age a framework of New life and Love that has never existed before, but which, when born in being in Man's world, will change the very vibrations in which he moves and has his being.

Then man, if he believes, can become a giant among men. And his knowledge and Wisdom can spread across the Heavens and open doors of which he knows not at this time.

Is it not worth it—Listen then, to the Higher Teachings, Oh Man! *Look up!* Reach up and gain the knowledge of the Spheres. For as you look and believe, so then, will you *become!* . . . And so it is."
Received by Bonnie Ireland   **—Captain Arcturus**

"Reason Enough To Get In Tune"

"The fact that there is a Major Cyclic Periodocity occurring just now, is reason enough to get in tune with the raising of the vibrations of Earth and every form and every aspect of *God's* Creations. Great changes are taking place, and will continue, for it truly is to be a 'new dispensation,' or perhaps I should say, 'a new schoolroom.' "
Received by Omar   **—Raymere**

"I AM from Inner Space!"

"I am not from outerspace entity, *I AM from inner space!*"
Channeled by J.Z. Knight   **—Ramtha**

"Self Governing—Self Sovereign —Self Sufficient"

"There are coming days that being self governing, to be self sovereign and self sufficient will be those that will live through the drama* that is fixing to occur, as it is now seen. And of course not possessing those qualitites is a very good indicator of how much you don't love yourself, and you depend on others for your support.
(* for a detailed elaboration see the video entitled "Change, The Days To Come," Ramatha Dialogues)

To be self willed, is to be self governed. A wise entity understands—that in economic collapse what will be of value shan't be stocks, bonds, certificates. They'll have no meaning. That which is rideable, that which is edible, that which is liveable, that which is growable, that is where value will be. And that is really a wondrous hour that comes. War of Valued Life creates that which is called the coming back to moments of simplicity for the complexities of social consciousness. It sort of wrings out the impurities and stabilizes that which is pure.

Being a simple entity is being a survivor. Being simple allows self love to occur. If the only thing you know is how to go to your supermarkets, and choose and pick and complain at every little corner, you have a very shocking awareness coming. For you shan't be able to *do that!*

In this that now I have put forward there will be fear that will run rampant in the market place in varying degrees. And there will be capitalists that will do very well as a result of it. In some areas I will control it because that which I AM has the power to do that. And yet it is of that knowledge that one can start the preparation of what is to come *now,* before you can no longer leave.

There is always the probability and the existence of change in destiny because Godman is endowed with free will and it is through the free will that at any moment *He* can interact, engage, and rediscover *Value! At any given moment!!!* It is in all equal understanding possible, that that which has delved so deep into mass, into decadence, can have a revival. That is possible for everyone. But the denser it becomes the more ominous the stratum is looking. All you have to do is to smell and look up and if you can't see the sun, it is happening masters. As it is known now all things are in order and they are getting ready to make their appearances. At any moment it can change. But *know you* what that would take

from mankind to give up his power??? And the iniquities of himself, to give up wanting to be outrageous? When man becomes a limited creature he is the most limited there is! For not even the animals of the Earth possess that stature of limitation."
Channeled by J.Z. Knight   **—Ramtha**

Sananda Speaks on "Fear"

"Beloved Ones:—This day let us speak of 'fear'—fear being that which comes for the reason thou knowest not the 'Plan.' The Plan is fashioned for the *good of all,* yet when one is given over to fear of any kind, it is for the unknowing, the darkness which prevails upon the Earth—that mist which man hast created for himself—the 'fog-mist' which shall be put aside, when they have asked for Light. I say, when they have asked for Light, the mist shall disappear and be *no more.* So be it that 'they' are filled with fear, they fear that which they comprehend not! They fear the Light, for they have fortuned unto themself great darkness, therefore they are more comfortable within their own environment. 'They' fear being removed from the environment which they have fortuned unto themself—they have no desire to reach up unto the greater heights."
Recorded by Sister Thedra   **—Sananda**

"Joy! Joy! Shall Fill The Earth!"

"Beloved of Mine Being: Wherein is it said, that I know the watering places of the Earth, and the deserts; all the places I *know.*

And the inhabitants thereof I know by name and number; by their light I know them, and they are no strangers unto Me;

for there are none indigenous of the Earth thereupon; they have had their origin in and upon another place which they left—or went out from long ago. There is a *fiat:* That they shall now return unto it, for a new people shall inhabit the Earth; and She too shall be made new, in preparation for to receive Her new residents; they shall take up their residence upon and within a new—clean and beautiful Earth; and She shall be joyful for Her release from bondage, and renewal; for long hast She been in bondage, and bondage, and renewal; for long hast She been in bondage, and crying for release. I say: The *new* residents shall be as ones which have been prepared to partake of *her joy* and release, for which there shall go forth a *great cry of joy,* and it shall manifest as a Great and Shining Light about the Earth, and it shall be seen from afar; and man shall navigate the seas by the light which is made manifest therefrom. I say unto thee: *A great* and *shining star* shall be the point of such heavenly *light;* and it shall shed its radiance about and above all the residences of the *new earth*—and they shall walk and weary not, for they shall be one with the *radiance.*

I tell thee of a surety—thou shall see and be *one* with *it;* and so great shall be thy joy—so great shall be thy *joy,* thou shall sing out: *"Praise the Father Solen Aum Solen, praise Him all ye host, praise him!! Joy! Joy!* shall fill the Earth! So let it *be*—for this have I spoken."

Recorded by Sister Thedra   **—Sananda**

"The Decision 'What You Want To Do' "

"If you know and have knowledge of, then you can always make the decision what you want to do. That eliminates fear. Being prepared as it were, eliminates being caught off guard, as it were, because being caught off guard is terrifying, I know I was a *Master Conqueror.*"

Channeled by J.Z. Knight   **—Ramtha**

"Have They Not Known The Same Sorrows, The Same Joys?"

"Mine Children: There are many which do stand guard for thee, while thou knowest not their part—I say unto thee: Ye know not their part—I say unto thee: These are thine Benefactors which ye know not. I say: Ye know not all thine Guardians, for ye have not remembered these thine Benefactors, which contribute their energy and their effort unto thine welfare—I say: They give of themselves that ye might be brought out of bondage. Now I say unto thee: Thine Benefactors labor long and tirelessly that ye be spared greater suffering and sorrow—while I say unto thee, they serve selflessly and with joy, asking nothing—giving all. Wherein have ye seen such service? I say unto thee, thou hast not!

Now I say unto thee: These thine Benefactors are thine Elder Brothers, which have gone before thee to prepare the way before thee. I say: They have overcome, and they know the same path which thou now walketh—for hast it not been given unto them to know the going and the coming—the going out and the coming in? And have they not known the same sorrows, the same joys? *Yet there are no joys like unto that of lifting up a younger brother,* and giving assistance unto him in the time of his trials—so be it the greater joy. I am One of these which know, for have I not come into the Earth for that purpose?"

—I AM the Lord God Sananda—be ye blest of Me and by Me, for I AM the Son of the Most High Living God. Amen and Selah.

Recorded by Sister Thedra

"You Shall Have Need
Of Your Stores and Provisions"

"These eons you have been told, the hour approaches. These eons you have been told, it is time to prepare. And yes, for eons you have been told to gather in thy stores. And what have you done? You have grown tired of these admonitions. You have grown weary in your preparation, and you have grown fat and lazy as you would go of your path. The hour is come. I speak not of an eon beyond thy eye. Nay, I speak not of this. I speak of the moment. The hour is come. Look at your preparation, what have you done? You have been told of the days of darkness. You have been told of the need to prepare. You have been told to gather in your stores, and I speak not of that now which feeds the spirit for I do speak of that which warms and brings comfort to the physical vehicle. This has been given to you. Have you done it? Have you done of this?

Might I offer up for your suggestion O noble ones of Earth, that you might consider gathering in your stores. You have been told that this shall be a season that shall be one of great unbalance. So be it, it shall. And you shall have need of your stores and your provisions, not only for your beloved ones, but you shall have need to assist of others. No, I say not to hoard, to deny one that another might gain, this is not my intent as I speak. I say to you to use wisdom in that which you do. Gather in your provisions that no effort, no thought from your vehicle might be wasted at such a time that higher thoughts are needed. Be as your mouse about the field. Does it not scurry here and scurry there that it would pick up, that it would gather in its stores to prepare for that time when it cannot scurry about the lands? So be it. Be as the mouse of the field, gather in that which you shall need.

Do you have candles that shall give you light? And do you have that which shall give you a measure of warmth? For you shall come into a season which shall be quite cold, and you shall need of the warmth. And yet there shall be ones that will pant as the sun beats down upon their heads, for they shall not need the warmth for they shall have too much. And do you have water? This potion is one that is necessary for your survival, for your vehicle does not function without this potion. Do you have water? See to it beloved ones, see to it. And so shall thy physical vehicle then be adequately prepared for, and be as one that is prepared.

And now we shall speak of the greater preparation, with your indulgence. Do you have sufficient word within your dwelling place that you might be able to read, to contemplate, to think only of that which is perfect, that will help you to rise up above your present situation. You shall have opportunity to learn if you have the ability to meditate in drastic situations. Can you fix your minds eye? Have you trained your thoughts sufficiently that you might put all that is around you from your consciousness, that you might be able to tune in where you have directed your thoughts? Have you evolved to this state beloved ones? Might I offer the suggestion that you work on this for you shall need of this sooner than you realize."
Received by Tuieta   **—Theoaphylos**

"Yet Where Will They Be"

"This light is not a new thing. Glimmers have appeared here and there through many at different points in time. Yet broadly speaking, it has not been a known thing either. Or perhaps it has appeared in distorted form. It has not been stressed or particularly emphasized by us until this generation. There are many present, even with the folds of New Age concepts, who will cry that these things must not be spoken of. Yet where will they be when the word is needed to comfort the hearts of millions, when the sky is darkened with space-craft, come to lift them to safety?

PHOTO BY KEVIN LAHEY

PHOTO BY MICHAEL RADFORD

So we must have our nucleus of messengers with the stamina and the courage to dare to get the message to the people of Earth, that this hour will come, and that when it does, there will be help ready in the skies to care for them! We do not involve ourselves with the dogmas of Earth or crystallizations of the doctrines of men. If our alerting messages or warnings or any portion thereof seems to be at odds with accepted traditional interpretations of things, then let tradition *update* its information by returning to *direct* contact with the *celestial government* of this solar system!

Souls of Divine Illumination will not be overcome with fear because of a foreknowledge of coming events, but will, rather, but filled with a joyous confidence in the Heavenly Father and take refuge in His shadow until these calamities be passed. This, then is your refuge from the storm, your shadow from the heat. With these revelations we share with you some of the details involved in the Father's Presence and the means with which it will be manifested in the crisis hour for the children of God. It is well to trust in the general principle that, 'come what may, God will take care of me.' It is even more comforting to be appraised of His method and His Plan for doing so.

In the darkest hour that can come for this planet, when its very existence would be destroyed were it not for the intervention of the Father's Hand, the millions who have dared to trust in Him when they had no other evidence other than their own faith, will be rewarded openly by being lifted into His Ark of Safety. As a hen gathereth her chicks under her wings, this ark provided will be the great armadas of floating cities that orbit the Earth on their *mission of mercy!*

—**I AM Kuthumi,** World Teacher of this Solar System
Received by Tuella

"Let Them Not Bind Thee"

"Ye shall arise—shake off thine legirons, and be ye free from all thine legirons, opinions, preconceived ideas, and let them not bind thee more, for it is given unto Me to see them bound fast by them. They are bound as by chains, which hold them within their tracks; they move not—for fear they do conform unto man's preconceived ideas his opinions—they are bound in their tracks and move not! I say: These are the ones which have been slaves of man's opinions and ideas—they seek signs and wonders, and run after them—seeking what? they know not!—they seek not after *light/wisdom/righteousness:*

Let them be reminded from whence cometh their help!—
the peace—for this have I spoken—so be it I am not
thru **I AM the Lord thy God Sananda."**
Recorded by Sister Thedra

"Because You Want Their Opinion"

"Do not allow yourself or any one else to make you think you are something that you are not!, because you want their opinion, you understand? Because it is, very easy to become that way if you embrace it just once then you're stuck. Then you don't know if you belong here or here or anywhere—because you set it into motion by allowing it to be there . . .

You have to change what you think about yourself and defy anyone else to allow their thoughts to make you what they want you to be. Love them for their truth but don't become it, if it isn't *you!*
Channeled by J.Z. Knight   —**Ramtha**

"A Brief Summary Of Your Initial Days With Us"

"Good evening ladies and gentlemen, my name is Aleva. For your convenience, dear ones, I shall spell this. It shall be A-L-E-V-A. I was informed it is now my turn that I might speak with you. Thank you for allowing me to come forth. I would be known to you of Earth as one of the Space People, though to us this does seem a strange way of referring to brothers and sisters. I have come from a distant planet, that I might assist you of Earth in the days to come.

It is my joy to tell you, that I am responsible for a group of guides for you of Earth, here on the various ships. You might refer to us as 'Big Brothers or Big Sisters' for we shall be with you as you come. We shall help you in your adjustment, help to answer many of your questions, and to ease your transition into this dimension of our ships. We have been assigned to groups of three to five individuals on Earth, that we might help you as you take your step from Earth to here.

Just as we have been assigned to you ones, we monitor your activities quite closely, that we might familiarize ourselves with your preferences, your manner of speaking, your thought patterns, and your 'personalities' so that we might make you as comfortable, as quickly as possible.

I am sure that there are many on Earth that are concerned of the eating patterns here on our ships. I am also sure you are concerned as to the manner of dress and what to expect. As we have sat in our various councils we have come to the conclusion that it might help you if we gave you a brief summary of your initial days with us as you come forth. With your permission I should like to do this at this time.

As you come forth, as you are beamed forth, you will enter into a room that to you would—like—full of equipment. You would stand there for a short time until your cellular activity has adjusted to our frequency rate.

At such a time then your guide would take you into a larger room, for there shall be many that will be coming forth. This would be, as you would call, an entry way, a grand hall or such. In this large room, you will find many with whom you are familiar. These shall be ones of Earth, and ones from the Higher Dimensions as well. This is a general mingling time, and to help you acclimatize yourself to your new surroundings, so that you will have no fear or apprehension.

Then after a short period you will be shown to your rooms, for a welcomed opportunity to refresh yourselves and to rest.

During your initial period with us, you shall be taken into that portion which we call our medical facilities, that you might receive of balancing, that certain sleeping portions of your brain might be activated so that thought communication can quite easily (be) established with each of you. No, this shall alter you in no way, and have no fear that we shall attempt any mind control, though I know this has been spoken of, on your planet. We do not use speech such as yours. Ours, our communication is through thought transference. All of you are quite capable of this, though there are portions of your brain that are quite sluggish because of long disuse. But as you shall be in our medical facility, you would be balanced, your frequency vibration would again be adjusted so that you would be comfortable.

You shall also receive classes both individual, and in small groups for those of you that would be coming back to Earth after the cleansing period.

Your manner of clothing while with us would be, how shall I say, it would be a one piece suit. The men and the women's suit would be basically be the same, and it would be in a color that would be coded according to your specific purpose. I am sure, just as we do, you shall find these suits quite comfortable.

For your convenience we shall have specific mealtimes where you of Earth might gather. Though I must say, we are endeavoring to have many of your foods with which you are familiar, you shall find that there are a large number that shall seem quite different to you. I would urge you to partake of these, for you shall find they are quite nutritious, and have quite a lasting quality. These shall be foods that have come from other planets, from other places within your universe. And some of the fruits you shall eat, for the first time, will be ones that you shall find on Earth when you return. You shall find that we have a beverage, that at your first taste, you would think of as your earthly wine. No, this is not so. We serve no alcoholic beverages, but you shall find this to be quite refreshing and relaxing.

Each of you, as I said, shall have classes individually, as well as in small groups with our beloved leaders, with the commanders within the Federation, and with specific ones of the Spiritual Hierarchy. Here again, this will be according to your purpose, and what your role is in the days to come. Many of you shall be returning to Earth, for your role is to help to build the New Earth. Your role is to help to parent the seeds that will come forth.

Others of you will have finished that which you have come to do, and you shall be returning to your home planets, your home stars. You shall be returning to distant galaxies, and others shall be ascending to yet another dimension.

As, I am sure you are aware, I feel such a joy to speak with you this evening. I have waited for this opportunity as I have been in service to the Radiant One. I eagerly await your arrival as do your other brothers and sisters. Thank you for allowing me to join with you this evening, and I shall look forward to the day when I might show to you the same gracious hospitality, that you have shown to me. Good night."

Received by Tuieta   **—Aleva**

"The Key—'You Have to Want God' "

"The keys that unlock the kingdom of heaven is called want! You will never be alive and be Godman until you want to, and never deviating from that desire for that is the fire within, that is the love that is the *LIGHT!!!* You have to want to have *you* back again. You have to want courage, you have to want simplicity, you have to want allowing what doesn't make you happy to flow from you. You have to want to live and you have to *want God,* the *is*— the Silver Wings, the Sunrise, the Wind on the Water, the Spice of Autumn. You have to want it!

That is up to you. The Will of God is possessed in Godman—which allows him his unique flavor. If you don't want it, and you want to slumber, and you want to be confused, and you want to be unhappy because 'you don't deserve happiness!'—first you don't even *know* what it is you deserve. Happiness doesn't mean anything here.* You keep wanting to get beyond that but you don't know what it is you are trying to get beyond. If you don't want to step out of your image and leave the hull behind, *you don't put the key in the door!*

Channeled by J.Z. Knight   **—Ramtha**
(* here—the physical body)

"The Secret of Attainment"

"The first step unto knowledge is desire; desire leads to action; action leads to attainment; attainment leads to wisdom, and there is the Secret to Attainment.

So be it that I am come that each and every one attain unto Wisdom for none shall be given the Key of Attainment without action, without preparation—and the preparation is the Key to Attainment—Attainment is the result of preparation —So be it and Selah."

—Sananda

"I Shall Send Teachers Among Them"

"Sori Sori—Now their land shall be laid waste, and nothing that has been built by the hand of man shall be left standing. It is for them to learn and know only that which is of Spirit will endure. They have not heeded My call to prepare themselves, and they shall be caught unaware, sleeping in their beds, and they shall find their preparation for comforts and security has been misplaced. Yet I shall send teachers among them during their time of trial, and they shall know the wisdom of My Words, So be it and Selah.

—Sananda

"The Victor"

"Hail, Hail unto the Victor! For he cometh forth as one which has overcome; he cometh forth as one arrayed in Light; he raiseth on wings of Light; he bears the authority of his own name. His number is written upon his garment; his authority is within the word of his mouth, for he hast the authority within his mouth. He has the Rod within his hand to give and to receive; he has the reign over the world; he has learned that which hast been said unto him—he hast overcome.

He has become one with the Light which hast become his Vesture. He hast control over the elements, for he hast become *one* with The Light."

Recorded by Sister Thedra   **—Sanat Kumara**

PHOTO BY MICHAEL RADFORD

PHOTO BY KEVIN LAHEY

CHAPTER SEVEN

CHRISTED BEINGS,

CHILDREN OF THE UNIVERSE
AND THEN
THE

SONG

"What is a Christ"

"What you are, to that which is termed, all that *is*, is in a staging processes called Christos. *Know you what the Christos is!* It is that which is termed, as it were indeed, God rising forth from a latent, dormant state within, that which is termed the genetic surviving humanity coming forward. It is indeed, that essence of one's entity self, that aparts it from all other creatures. It is called indeed, God arising in mankind. How *think* you!?, how *know* you!?, that you are intelligent, you are emotional, that you are decisive creatures without purpose!!! What *is a christ*, is when one rises above that, which is termed, the mundane, and that which is termed as it were indeed, the wholeness of humanity and their social struggles, you see? Christ is that which comes forth in unlimited outpouring measure. And the lot of you that are so gathered here, are each individual, that which is termed Christ—Godman.

The only way one goes beyond, that which is termed, the desperation and the illusions and the sorrow and the confusion in this life is to rise to that purpose. How many times do you want to come back? How many more lifetimes are you going to spin here on this plane? How many faces are you going to wear? How many circumstances are you going to create for yourself? How many more parents? How many more situations? How many more games? It is wholly up to *you!* Know you when you are finished with this level, when you have become greater than this level, that is indeed becoming a Christ?

A voice from the wilderness is heard and harkened to. One that lives its conviction of itself, *wholly of itself!* And often times denying that which is termed; family—that which is termed; creed doctrine—that which is termed; conviction of religion. Know you what keeps you from becoming that (Christ)? All of those things. That which is termed as it were indeed, the denial of social structures becomes very important. It is not that you are giving up something, and you're suffering the loss—it is that that which you are giving up no longer owns you and in fact you have become grander than it. The voice that cries from the wilderness doesn't come from the city—it does not come from that which is termed, the market place; nor is it written in your libraries. The wilderness, entity, is the unexplored area of your personal self. The voice, is a calling, as you would term it. It is a voice of subtle natures, it begins to say to you 'is it worth it?'—'do I love what I am?'—'am I indeed impeccable with who I am?'—'to what level, to what degree have I given up all of myself, only to engage that which is termed the priorities of my peers and its society?'

The Christ, the coming forth, the voice in the wilderness, this that speaks to you *is not outside of you!* I am outside of you. It is *inside of you!!!* It is a feeling, no it does not say to you in that which is termed, vocal tones 'you better get on with it least you be left out.' It does not say that. It in fact as it were indeed is a feeling 'are you who you really are?' Know you that to become a Christ is denying other's desires for you and beginning to listen to your own? That is what it is all here, this Kingdom here, to listen to you, for once, a moment, rathering to listening to the lot of everyone else. To find out what is *important!* What is important in your life? What are you creating here, *indeed!,* that you are possibly going to take with you hereafter? Not even the linen upon your back. It is all *within you.* What are you going to take with you? There is a rare essence within all of you to be more than Divine! To be more than splendid!"

Channeled by J.Z. Knight
—Ramtha

195

"The Christ Presence Within Each Soul"

"While great human need on a mass level prevails throughout the planet, I have observed the spending of vast sums of millions and millions of dollars of temples of stone that men might glory thereby, but these shall crumble in the dust. This ostintatiousness in My Name has grieved my heart again and again. I did not give My Life for such as this. I did not come to be made into a god. I came as one of you, to show you the Divine Possibilities that abide within every human life. I came to show the Way, the Path, the Truth, but the world has chosen to exalt Me and My Name but to ignore and forsake My Teachings of the inner kingdom.

There has come One to take up My Work within the hearts of humanity. The Christ Presence within each soul, continues to lead and to show the Way. This is My Contact and My Outreach to every soul upon the planet. As you pay homage to the Christ Presence within your neighbor and your brother, you pay homage to Me and My Words. As you extend the Love of God around your planet to all in need of that Love, you extend your Love to Me. There is so much talk of Christianity upon the Earth, but so little of the Presence of the spirit of Christ. Churchianity abounds and divisions compound within it. But there is so little of My Teaching in action in the life of humanity.

But all of this will change as the Earth is born into a New Day. Exterior religion will fall away and inner awareness will become the strength of those who follow Me. I shall walk with them and be in their midst, for they shall endure."

—I AM Esu known to Earth as Jesus the Christ
Received by Tuella

"Why Do You Worship Me, Why Did You Ever Worship Me?"

"You do not reach the son through its mother, you reach the son through the *Son*, not his mother, I came to fulfill a prophecy."

☆ ☆ ☆

"What are prophecies? They are the hopes that are now seen, they are the envisionments."

☆ ☆ ☆

"O man, o man, in all your peril, in all your Divine confusion, you have all done to yourselves the right for damnation."

☆ ☆ ☆

"To bring forth peace to the world, was to fulfill the prophecy of *hope*, and to outlive the conspirators, to outlive them!"

☆ ☆ ☆

"My life as told by you was greater and more humble than what you have heard, and little for the reason on that you have heard."

☆ ☆ ☆

"Why do you worship me, why did you ever worship me, perhaps because I fulfilled a prophecy, because I did wondrous works that your blind eye would not permit you to see in your own doing. Why did you worship me, because only I had the strength, the knowingness to *be!* To teach the Glory of God in *His* perfect Kingdom—which lies not within the grand temple but in the rock of Peter, and in the depth of his innocence and in his pure Virtue."

"That is how the Kingdom of Heaven *is*, in the simplest of things and of measure—My Life I already chose, I was the Herald of Peace, I was the Star, I was the Angel that called my brothers the shepherds . . ."

☆ ☆ ☆

"As I grew, so did My awareness—what is called man in his hell grew. And where did I get My Knowledge?—I brought it with Me, I never forgot—*I never forgot.* I decided to come unto this plane to exhibit a prophecy, not to My peoples but *all peoples!!!* Even Ceasor in his silken bed. And what is the knowledge?—That where God be, it does not lie in the 'scriptures,' or in the grand temples! or in the Holy covenant! *It lies within!*—The fire is *within*—God is with His allegiance with man, His covenant is within him!"

☆　☆　☆

"Life is grandeur than the grape, or the cross, or the fire, Life has no ending!"

☆　☆　☆

"It was not that you believe on Me, but that you believe in that which is *within you!* The Greater freedom, the Greater knowingness, and giving examples of *life!* Not Me—I am nothing without the God within Me—Alone I am nothing, I alone can do nothing—without God within Me, the Father within me. As you alone can do nothing without the *Father* within you! What was the miracle? Love *is* the miracle!"

☆　☆　☆

"Why do you not know? Why do you not know? That if a great tree who's roots go deep into the Earth, and looses all of it's pungent leaves—dies in the winter and yet comes back in the spring, and yet lives again, and the wheat that is cut down in the height of its glory and yet returns in the spring. Why are those things greater and more important than *you??* You will not die. Going back unto your mother's womb, and you will but you will not die. Be trouble with this, and trouble with this and they succored to My tombs and mourning garments and nungents and oils and prayed long for their dead! Why do you not know?—that you are greater than the tree who lives in spring and you are greater than the grasses that return in the wheat on the stalk and the flower in the new bloom, why do

☆　☆　☆

"You are never to be in worship, you are to *be enlightened!* And to understand *God,* not as the 'scriptures' have taught Him to be—but what *He is within you!* My kingdom what was it? My kingdom existed of twice robes, sandals, and bread. That was My kingdom—*My Glory* was *within Me,* and no cross or judgement could take it from me. What I have taught you lives within you still, you do not have to crucify that which loves you any longer, but love that which loves you. And it is not I, I alone am nothing—it is the God *within* Me that *loves* you, and *always has!"*
Channeled by J.Z. Knight

—Jesus

"Awaken Unto Thine True Identity"

¢ ¢ ¢ "—Art thou not aware of thine self? Art thou not aware of *being?* Art thou not aware of thine Divinity? I say unto thee, because thou art Divine thou dost have thine being within the Father which has sent thee forth as a part of Himself—as the hand, the foot extended. He hast the power and the will to move it forth; to bring it back; to do that which He will that which He hast sent forth.

As thou dost stretch forth thine hand of thine own 'free will' thou art able to withdraw it, thrust it forward and withdraw it—therein is motion and energy, set into motion of thine own will. Now I say unto thee, the Father hast sent thee forth as Himself—as one made flesh, and as one projected of Himself. And He shall bring thee forth as He Wills, for it is His Will that ye be at *one* with Him. And at no time hast thou been separate from Him—yet thou hast not been aware of thine Source, the Source of thine being.

It is now come when ye shall become aware of thine Divinity, and ye shall be glad, for it is thine 'Salvation.' I say unto thee, it is thine deliverance from bondage—thine unknowing, which hast bound thee in darkness. So be it I say unto thee, 'Be ye aware of thine Divinity,' for it is given unto thee to be Eternal Beings, and of Divine Origin.

For this have I spoken unto thee, that ye might *know*— that ye might become *aware* of thine *source.* So let it be for thine own sake that I say unto thee, 'Awaken unto thine true Identity.'

Recorded by Sister Thedra   **—Hilarion**

"To Be Unison With The Lord God That You Are"

"And at this time I would say to you the Lord God of that which I AM, which is of the Lord God of the Totality, comes forth to greet you in harmony and to be unison with the Lord God that you are. Now my brethren, Ramtha, has spoken of the Lord God of your totality, the Lord God of your being. And for some this is a term that is quite unfamiliar, for you are yet to accustomize yourselves to the thought that you have Christos within you. And we shall speak of this. For ye ones need to know of your Divinity. Too long you have been schooled, you have been taught that God is out there and you are in here. And never the twain shall touch until that time that you leave of this plane, you develop wings and you start flying and playing harps. This has been your teaching. From the small child upward this has been your teaching.

But there is a spark that is awakening. There are lessons from the mouth of the Divine. For they do come forth and say to you, 'You are Divine. You are beautiful. You are of the Perfect.' Did you know of this? Do you feel of this within your heart? You have this right you know. You have this right.

Give the gift of love to the Christ that you are. Do not be afraid to love this Divine Portion that is you. Recognize this as your Lord God, as you walk about. And let this state of consciousness guide your every thought, your every word, your every deed. Let it be each breath that you breathe. So great shall be your enlightenment. So wondrous shall you be."

Received by Tuieta   **—Theoaphylos**

"A Specific Energy Pattern"

Question: "We notice that Sananda and Lord Maitreya use 'thee, thou, ye, etc.' Is there a specific purpose for this?"

"Greetings beloved ones, I am Monka to return. And I would take this opportunity to reply to your question. Oh yes, there is specific reason why 'thee, thy, myne,' are used for these are words that cannot be twisted, cannot be abused in your current earthly words, in your current earthly thinking. But these carry specific energies and specific thoughts with them. And though you of Earth have your grammatical way of presenting certain facts and presenting your information, that which is shared by the Hierarchy, and in some instances that which is shared by us is shared not in a grammatical manner that is peculiar to Earth, but it is shared to bring forth a specific cosmic energy that might ring forth to each individual that receives of the word. You will note also, as you read some of the words that have come that there are peculiar spellings in certain instances. Here again this carries a specific energy pattern with it, and this is a cosmic energy that goes beyond the grammatical acceptance of Earth. I trust this has answered your question. And I thank you for asking it for I know it has been on the tips of the tongues of others."

Received by Tuieta   **—Monka**

PHOTO BY SISTER THEDRA

PHOTO BY MICHAEL RADFORD

"To Communicate in Different Ways with Different Ones"

"We have the ability to communicate in different ways with different ones, and to do this at the same time. And we also have the ability to give the same message out to different ones around your Earth, and yet to deliver this message in a manner that is compatible with their acceptance. For you see there are ones upon your planet this hour that would not be comfortable with this discussion, for it would frighten them. So we come through and we speak in a different way to these ones, for we wish to frighten no one."

Received by Tuieta   **—Hatonn**

Children of the Universe

"The Cosmos is filled with life . . . in many forms . . . in myriads and millions of manifestations of the Creator's Hand. It is beautiful to behold all of His Marvelous Works.

We desire that Mankind shall look upon the heavens and behold it's wonders and realize that he too is a part of the Universe of Life . . . that he too has his part and inheritance with the Stars.

The millions who thus fill the space above you are but as a drop in the ocean or the grain of sand that rims it's edge. Man is not insignificant but is important within the framework of all the manifested children of the Father.

Man bears the imprint of Divinity within his being that will not be denied its birthright. Though slow the progression may sometimes be, nevertheless the mark of the Godhead is within man, to be brought forth as the bud of the flower that turns its face to the sun. So man will inexorably find his Divine Pathway back to the Stars and the many dimensions that await his coming."

Received by Tuella   **—Sanat Kumara**

"When You Ac-Knowledge Your Divinity?"

"There is no difficulties, there is indeed no illusion so powerful that it can take you from that *light*. God, that which is the within power, brings forth the Christ, that which is Godman resurrected. It is through the Christ and the Love of God that Godman is lifted out of the dreams to awaken. Because it is the power within you, that have created your limitations. You gave them power, it is up to you to lift yourself beyond them. And there is not one entity, within this August body, that does not have the power to do that, you understand?

To give credence to the Lord God of your Being, to speak of the Father within, is to acknowledge the divinity within. When you acknowledge your divinity you are without limitation, understand?"

Channeled by J.Z. Knight   **—Ramtha**

"Direct-Lines-Of-Contact"

"So it would be, that those who are of Earth and her sub-planes, who are open to the *spirit of truth*, are direct-lines-of-contact from the *higher* to the *lower*, and are faced by those who challenge from the *lower*. This is why it was said, that families would turn upon their own, for there are those who are in their ignorance, prompted by the *oppressors*—and who by their lack of *wisdom* turn upon those who seek only to bring *Christ* into a darkened world . . . and even those who seek to do *right*, in moments of weakness, can be prevailed upon to *react* in a manner below their aspiration.

It is well that you *realize*, the end of the struggle nears—and in its final throes, the clash between *forces* is strongly felt by *all*. The greatest struggle of a dying force comes at its final moments.

Truth has its edge, and gains in its *strength*. The *War of powers* and *principalities* shall soon subside, and man shall find his *peace*.

Christ comes as a light that shineth and darkness shall cease!!

With armies of Heaven, and warriors of earth
CHRIST SHALL REIGN !!

Transcribed by Teska   —**I AM Esu**—called Jesus"

"The Beauty of Our Ever-Evolving Process"

"Good morning beloved sister. I am Andromeda Rex speaking.

As you gaze out your window and watch the rain feel the gratefulness of the nature kingdom for its nourishment and sustenance. As the sun comes forth each shall lift its head with renewed brightness. This is a reflection of its joy and thanksgiving. The blessed element of water feeds and cleanses as it comes to Mother Earth. It takes away that which is harmful and replaces it with the purity of the living waters of life. It takes up that which is not good to return it to the Cosmos, to be changed and charged in love. Such is the beauty of our ever-evolving process. Such is the wonder that as yet has escaped the mind of man.

As man progresses along his path he shall begin to feel more of an at-one-ment with all of the forces of nature and its many and diversified kingdoms. He shall learn of the peace of harmony with all of creation. As he learns this, doors shall begin to open that have here-to-fore been closed to him. He shall see with new eyes and he shall truly feel wonder at what he beholds. Our man of earth as a collective unit has followed for many embodiments the love of the self or the 'I.' He has not recognized that the greatest mastery is one of harmony

and living with all of creation. Is not this the lesson that our Radiant One gave to man when he was in embodiment as Jesus? He claimed no glory of his own. He came to you as a living example of all that was yours if you lived the laws of the Divine Creator, yet too, too few truly recognized what he spoke. Too few heard his real message. Then as now man looks for him to return to smite the enemies and to prove that one was right and the other wrong. They look to him to elevate the individual as he puts down another. Over all of these your earth years, few have truly heard his teachings. Truly the loss is man's, for to be with this one, our beloved leader and teacher is to truly feel all of what his words of teaching did convey. Man has but to be in His Presence but a fraction of a second and the effects can and do stay him throughout eternity. I welcome the day for all of mankind when they might have opportunity as we have to sit with Him. I am your brother of space signing off."

Recorded by Tuieta   —**Andromeda Rex**

"To Feel As I Feel"

"Our beloved Commander-in-chief is presently with us, and the joy and the Light that is sent forth from this most precious one, truly, is a blessing of untold bounty to each of us who have opportunity to sit in this presence. I know each of you look forward to the moment when you may do the same, just as I when a small lad, did eagerly await these moments. If I could ask for man the supreme joy, I would ask for him to be able to feel as I feel, when in the presence of the Radiant One. Forgive my impatience, but eagerly I seek for man of Earth, the

204

love and the joy and peace we are able to experience.

I beg of you, your indulgence, but it is imperative that man of Earth in his grossly material world, raise his vibrations, that he might come forth to the everlasting love of the Divine Creator. Cast away your chains of possessions and your worship of these. Free yourselves that you might rise to walk in the new day."

Received by Tuieta   **—Monka**

and I shall come unto thee as One which hast been thine Comforter. And I shall be evermore with thee, for I forget thee not in thine slumbers, and wanderings.

I forget thee not, yet too I say: Remember ye *me,* and I shall speak unto thee gently and surely. Put forth thine hand, and know that I AM closer than thine hand—for in *me* thou hast thine Being—nothing is hidden up from Me."

—So be it I AM thine **Mother Eternal**

Recorded by Sister Thedra

"Spirit Quickens Flesh"

"Sarah Speaking—

Mine Children: I am speaking unto thee as Mine Own. At no time have I forgotten thee; I know thine every need; no, I know thine longings, and for this do I come unto thee this day. I come, for it is given unto Me to know thine longings, and I come that they be fulfilled; that ye no more be sorely distressed; that ye no more hunger and yearn for thine fulfillment—for in Me ye shall find fulfillment, for I am thine Eternal Mother and I hold thee fast. I bring unto thee the fulfillment of thineself—yet thineself is not flesh, neither the desires of flesh; I say flesh is the lesser part, it is the lesser.

While the fulfillment is not flesh, it is not to be understood what is meant by 'fulfillment' thru flesh, for flesh hast not the capacity for fulfillment; neither can, nor does it comprehend the meaning of the fulfillment of Spirit. While Spirit quickens the flesh, and makes ready for the fulfillment, it remains yet unknown unto thee the meaning of fulfillment.

Awaken unto Me, and I shall bring unto thee comfort; and ye shall be as ones comforted, for I say unto thee, I am the Comforter, for I AM thine Mother. I hold thee close, I succor thee in the time of need—I forget not Mine Own. I place within thine hand Mine; hold ye fast and be ye as a little child,

"Life Was Created For Glory and Beauty"

"Humans have allowed their thinking brains to not think. Not only do they not use their capabilities to a great extent but they . . . are robot-like in their thinking and actions. Life was created for the glory and beauty. Disregard of this is not allowed. From the trees out to the moon, stars and planets, there is no place a human can walk, see, or just be that is not a thing of beauty. That which is not beautiful is from his doing."

Received by Ann Valentin   **—Silver Ray**

"In the Higher Mansion Realms"

"Now, for those who are illumined in Light, we give the higher impetus of the Christ Ray as the Christ enfolds and instills His Ray within each individual Being. Those who have the Christ Ray within will receive a greater illumination and those that are just receiving it, will receive the Light of the Christ on those frequencies that they can withstand. Each day as they gain in Light, they shall receive a greater impetus of the most glorious ray and become themselves a Christed

Being as I myself became. And what I have become, you also can become, and what I do, you also can do and even more as you unite with our Father-Mother in the Higher Mansion Realms, as you walk with me and the Buddha, with the Mother into the Solar Energies of Being. In doing so, you will begin to see and function with the Masters, with me on a face to face personal basis, yet in greater oneness of Light exchange, of Love, than you have ever known before. Eventually you shall see Our Radiant, Glorious *I AM that I AM,* Father-Mother God, face to face and be filled with His energies and surrounded with His Being as a Star-Child within His Body, within the Sea, the Crystalline Sea of All Creation!

This is your destiny even while you are on the Earth-plane, if you so choose. You may work upon the Earth but yet upon the Mansion Realms at the same time if you so choose to raise and illumine and transform your Being into the beautiful Star Christed Being that you are, that you were in the Beginning and are now if you can but know and see and believe.

Each day ask to be filled with the Light and it shall be done. In your daily meditations, ask for greater illumination and you will be given the Light daily: The Crystalline Light, the White Light, the Golden Light, and each Ray of the Day shall fill your Being, your Chalice, to overflowing so that you will have enough to give unto others with your Love and with the Father's Love, with my Love, with the Love of all the Entire Spirit of the Great White Brotherhood and the Legions of Light, who work with us always thru the Father's glorious Plan of Love and Light and coevolution that His Will be done on Earth as it is in Heaven."

Received by Camhael   **—I AM Sananda Esu**

"Will Sananda Be Returning To Earth?"

Question: "Will the one that we knew as Jesus, that we know as Sananda be returning to Earth in the physical form as stated in the book of Revelations?"

"I am Monka to reply, and I am warmed at the opportunity to share of thoughts with you. May I say in one word dear brother, he has not left. He has not left your plane for he constantly monitors, he constantly ministers with, through, and for all ones of planet Earth. You of Earth, particularly of your particular western civilization, have been tied into various philosophical beliefs since the Beloved One has been upon Earth. Indeed as you have traveled your paths of truth, as each of you has sought in your own way to grow, you have been most diligent. Many ones of you have been most devoted in following the teachings of your various churches and that which you would call your religious denominations.

With your indulgence and permission I will add some thoughts for your consideration. As you think about, as you ponder of the return of this one that is known to you as Jesus, there are several factors that are involved in this return. One is each of you within your own total entity is a Christ. Now this is something that is not particularly palatable to your way of thinking, for you have received a beautiful indoctrination to the contrary. Just as, the Beloved One has been quoted to say that he died for your sins. And he said to you that he doesn't need your sins, they're yours alone. You must recognize that this one that was known to you as Jesus spoke of many things, and he spoke of them not as Jesus the man, but he spoke of them as that One which is the Christed Station. The interpretation by many ones of Earth has been that, 'Jesus said this . . . ' or 'Jesus said that . . . ' Jesus the physical form was the vehicle through which the Christ spoke and worked. This vehicle had been attuned to such a degree that it was in absolute harmony with the Christed Energies. This is where

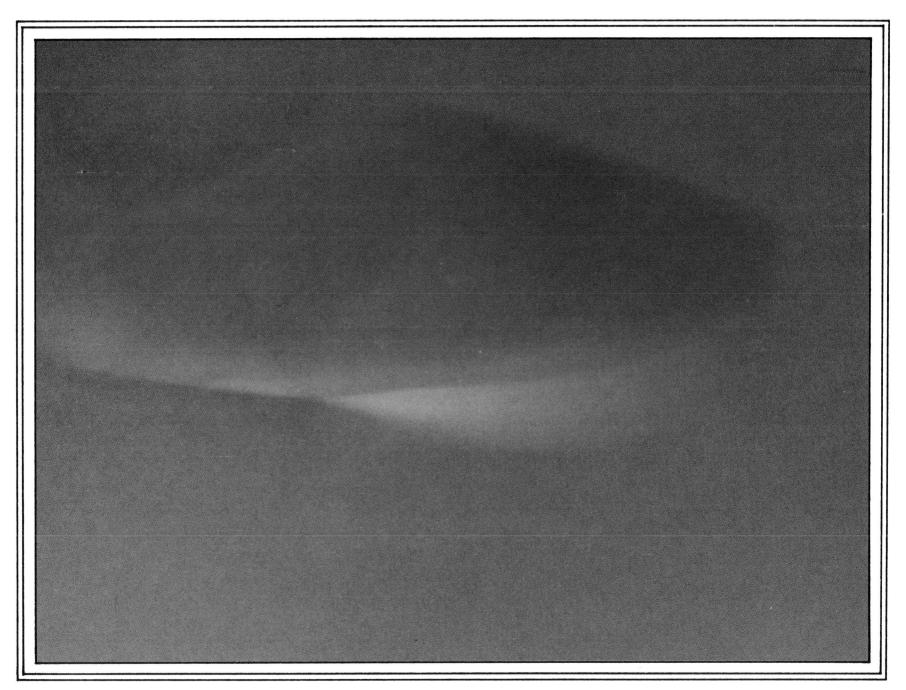

PHOTO BY MICHAEL RADFORD

most of you of Earth have difficulty. Though you have this same seed, this same ability within you, you are not, you have not, you have chosen not (and here I underline the word chosen), you have chosen not to attune yourselves to the point that the dear one known to you as Jesus did. Thus, that which is known as the Christ within your being does not find as easy an access through you as it did through him.

And so as it was spoken of that he would return to Earth, he would walk of Earth, this is so. The Christ does walk of Earth. He walks within each of you. That which is the Christed walks within each of you. And the Beloved One who has grown beyond the proportion of Jesus, who is the composite of the total energies of the Christed Station, who has achieved this dimension, this growth because of the life of the one that was known to you as Jesus, this one that we speak of as Sananda, our beloved leader, our guide, our Commander-in-Chief. Yes, he shall be on Earth. He shall be seen on Earth, just as he has been seen on Earth, and just as he has walked on Earth. But may I offer a thought for your consideration? Unless your eyes are opened and you are attuned, you will not see him. You must look for him, and as you look for him so will he reveal himself to you. I trust that in my answer that I have shared thoughts with you that would stir an awakening within you, that would cause you to ponder, that would cause you to think and would cause you to grow in your own Christed Portion. Thank you for your question."
Received by Tuieta — **Monka**

"I Shall Appear Here—I Shall Appear There"

"It is that I have cum unto the land. And I have cum to walk with thee. And to sup with thee. And I have cum to be kno-n by many. And many shall see my face. And they shall proclaim of mine arrival. So be it. It is that I have cum unto the land that I might see, that I might give sustenance to ye ones who do carry of the heavy load, that I might for a time share of this burden that is thine as ye do go forth in my name. It is that I have cum. And I say to thee, each and every one, go ye forth and say to them, 'He has cum. He has cum. Our Lord has cum. Rejoice with us and share in the feast. And kno he has cum.' This I would say to ye ones of Light. This I would say shall be the word that ye would give to them. This shall be thy word. And kno ye *ye speak truth* for *I AM cum.* I am cum unto the land. And many shall see my face. And I shall be kno-n by many names. But I say in truth my name shall be but one. And my name is Lord for I do cum as the Father-Mother God has bid me enter to walk with thee.

And I shall appear here. I shall appear there. In each far corner shall I appear. Kno ye I have cum. And in these places that do weep and cry and wail in the battle I shall be. Yea I am, for I have cum forth to give comfort to the mother who weeps at the loss of the son. And I have cum forth to give comfort to the father who lost of the son. And I have cum to give of my sustenance to each that would receive. And I have cum to share of the peace of the Cosmos with all that would share of the peace with me. I have cum unto the land that does cry and does weep. And I have given of this portion of the land of my peace. And I have gone forth with the merchants and the bankers and the ones of the mighty cartels. And I do sit with these ones and I do share with them of the love that is our Divine inheritance. And I do say to them—look ye only for that which is fair. Be not one caught with greed. Be not one to climb the back of another that ye might be above them.

Love ye one another. Love ye one another. Hold forth the hand to the widow who asks for the cup of milk. Give unto her ten times that which she does ask of you. And so shall you gro in your riches. And so shall your coffers be filled. These are mine words to these ones called bankers and merchants, these ones of the cartels. And I do go and I shall seat with the kings and the rulers. And I shall say to them, there is but one ruler. The Blessed Divine One that has created All. There is but One ruler.

Kno these ones that are within the boundaries of your governments are there by Divine choice. And they are there as a trust for you. O' you rulers of Earth that think yourselves wise, that see of your own wisdom, look beyond your small boundaries to that which is greater. Kno that not one portion upon this jewel may shine more brightly than the next but all of this gem shall glo in equal brilliance as it does cum forth. And there shall not be one spot within the gem that is not Light. And there shall not be one spot with the gem that shines more brightly than another for each is equal in the eyes of the Father-Mother God. And each has equal opportunity to cum forth and to be Light. This I would say to the kings and the rulers of your governments. And to these ones that scurry about, I would say—hear of my word. Receive of me. Ye have been as ones to spout of thy love. Ye have been as ones to proclaim of thy allegiance to me. And ye have been as ones that have most patiently gone into your churches each Sabbath day. And kno that I have cum. *Do you recognize me?* Do you see me for who I am? O' ye small ones that do scurry, few, few do see me and recognize me. Too few I say, for ye are as ones to look for me as I was yesterday. Open thine eye that ye might see me of this day. I cum not in flowing robes. I cum not with the staff and sandals upon my feet. Nay, nay that time is passed. But I cum just as you are this day. Can you not see me? Can you not feel my closeness? Can you not see I am not hidden within the churches, within these mighty buildings. O' nay, I am not bound to these places, for *I AM cum.* I am here to walk beside thee. And I am here to take thy hand and lead thee into the higher spheres. Open thine eye. O' children can you not hear me? Too many, too many have turned deaf ear to

mine word but the hour is that they shall not stop me. And they shall not stop my ones of Light, for my ones of Light do kno of my closeness. And we do share of the true communion. And these ones do kno I am with them and they do feel of the love that is ours to share. Kno ye as I do share with these ones of Light so do I share with all that would receive of me. And as each does receive of me so shall they share with another. For this is of the Plan. And this is of our purpose that all might cum forth. Now it is I do say to thee I am cum. In thy heart feel my closeness. Open thine eye that ye might see my face. Open thine ear that ye might hear mine voice. And lift thy heart that ye might receive of me."

Selah Om ni di eno cum eta

Received by Tuieta   **—Sananda**

"When He Says 'I Have Come,' Know That He Has Come"

Question: "On the instructions we have been receiving lately, Sananda has said to go tell them, 'I am cum. Thy Lord Sananda has cum.' For us ones of Earth can you give us some guidance as to how we can do that?"

"As you have been told. There is one thing you of Earth have yet to learn, for you have forgotten what it is like to be with the Beloved One, to be in his presence, or to be on the same ship that he is on. When our Lord, Commander-in-Chief Sananda speaks, all of the fleet hear his words, and feel the love that comes with these. And when he says to you, 'Tell them I have come,' He has come. His energies are on the Earth at this hour. They are on the Earth in greater concentration than they have ever been. And dear ones, my brother and I would say to all of you, remember he can be with you, and he can be here, and he can be in many places at one time. And when he says I have come know that he has come. Does this help?"

Received by Tuieta   **—Hatonn**

"Only Those That Are Firm And Rooted In the Truth Shall Stand"

"Good morning Tuieta. It is Beatrix returning. Blessings to you and to all that read these words.

This is a time of great sorting for you of Earth. There have been many up to this period that have dabbled in their interest of the higher teachings. Many of these have entered the door through the astral belt or the curiosity of magic and the unexplained. Theirs has not been a search but a game. They have been led to the higher teachings. These ones are now tiring of the demands that are placed upon them. They tire of no rapid materialistic manifestations. They want 'proof' on their level in their dimension or else. They feel that they can threaten the higher forces and succeed. Such a pity! Such a pity! They have not travelled with faith as their companion and now they are lost. So be it. So be it.

It is now that these ones shall be sorted away from those that truly search along the higher road. They shall be sorted from those that have made a commitment, have given of their choice. They shall be sorted. This is as has been given to you in the prophecy of ages past. You have been told that you will be sorted and sorted again; that only the pure will remain to inherit the new Earth as it bursts forth in its beauty. These ones shall go into a place that is more to their liking and their attunement. May they go in peace and rise up to the joy that is their Divine Inheritance.

Now for you ones that are 'surviving of the sorting' to this point, be strong and be sure for there shall be many forces about you that shall try to sway you. Be strong and sure. From our vantage view we see the storms that are churning the etheric about Mother Earth. We see that which comes to you as it lashes at you and you are tossed about. Only those that are firm and rooted in the Truth and are surrounded with the Golden Mist shall stand. Only those of you that are filled with the Light of the Divine Principle shall withstand the storms that are about you. We send forth our love and energy to help you to be strong. We send forth energy that you might use to tie yourselves into the Golden Light of the Christed One. May the peace and the joy that we have, come to blanket you against the upcoming storms. My words may seem to be a trifle dramatic but this is actually what we are observing."

Received by Tuieta   **—Beatrix**

"A Hand That Ye Too Be Lifted Up"

"While it is given unto Us of The Mighty Council to be above the law of the lower realms, it is given unto Us to be qualified to direct thee aright, that ye too come into the place wherein there is no limitation; wherein there is no bounds, no boundaries, no sorrow, no longing. Hast it not been said that thou shall be unbound? It is so—and it is given unto Us to know such joy. It is given unto Us to see the misery and sorrow of them bound in darkness. It is for Our knowing, and Our Love for thee that We give unto thee a hand that ye too be lifted up."

Recorded by Sister Thedra

211

"To Encourage and Uplift and Enlighten"

"Greetings. It is good to have an opportunity to come forth when we are in your sector, to speak a few words. It is always with pleasure that we also look down on you Eartheans who are in little groups. There may be different levels of awareness in each group. There may be different members, even of each group that are on different levels or grades of understanding but believe me, each one has our love and our blessings and always our hand to help uplift them if they will only create and keep that desire in their hearts and strive to put it into manifestation—in their thoughts, actions, and deeds. We need examples, we need teachers, we need new light coming into, even in the Kindergarten Grades. And we know that many seeds are being planted upon the earth plane. We are striving to do our part to encourage and uplift and enlighten to the greatest extent possible, each and everyone who has that desire to be an instrument or a channel."

Received by KaRene   **—Korton**

"This Is Truly A Time of Bountiful Harvest"

"Good morning, Tuieta. It is Mary to speak. I would this hour speak of all that lies before you and before man. From my vantage point much has already transpired on the etheric plane that is now coming to Earth. The cleansing has begun and man is at a crossroads for he can straighten of his back or he can bow down to all that which is about him. That which is about him at this hour is a heavy burden but it is one that cannot be carried by all of mankind. It is the burden of only a few. It is a burden that is not to be carried by all. You of the Light must concentrate your efforts and your energies on all that is good, all that is of the Perfect. You must in the midst of all that, that is raging about you, be of the Absolute. You must see all of the raging storm but do not be touched by it. You of the Light at this hour shall find the only solace is that of the love of our Lord Sananda. Do not place your allegiance to ones on the earthly plane for in the final hours you may find these ones do not have the strength to continue. Be strong and certain within your own hearts. Do not follow blindly or foolishly but give of your trust to those ones that are truly the messengers sent from the Divine One. At this hour as the energies are greatly concentrated to you ones of Earth, many shall feel they are receiving communications from the dimensions about the Earth. Be guardful of that which they do say and that they do claim. Be ever watchful and do not be taken in by false prophets who profess of their great worth. Kno just as our beloved one came in simple raiment so do his messengers. They make of themselves no claim. They come to deliver that which they were given. Theirs is not of the self but of the Word as it is given through them. Be cautious dear ones. Be cautious. This is a time of change and a time of great energies for all of the ones of Earth. Rejoice at what is shared so freely with you. Accept this gift that is so freely given. This is truly a time of bountiful harvest as all the goodness of the love of the Perfect One is given forth to bathe you and this small planet. Feel the love, accept the love, share the love that is so abundantly shared with you. Walk in the Light of the Holy of Holies this day as you go forth."

Selah Om ni de eno   **—I AM Mary**
Received by Tuieta

PHOTO BY MICHAEL RADFORD

"Action—Real Action!—Alive!—Vital"

"Beloved Ones: This day let it be said that the time is come for greater revelation—the populace shall no longer be bound in darkness concerning the things which are of greater import—they shall become aware of these things.

For this are We of the Mighty Host prepared—for We shall move as One Mighty Body—as One Mighty Company— and as One Mind as One Hand there shall be no confusion— no mistakes—for We are well schooled in Our part—and there shall be Action—Real Action! Alive!—Vital unto the welfare of the Earth and the inhabitants thereof.

There is no foolishness with this Body—this Company— this Plan—for it is a Serious Body—and all which comprise it are of One Mind. They know the Plan and They shall go forth in One Body—and Their parts shall be as the Plan has called for. They shall go at the appointed moment—and there shall be no delay, hesitation, or confusion on Their part—yet I say: there shall be confusion on the part of the ones which are found unprepared—for they shall be confused."

Recorded by Sister Thedra   **—I AM Sananda**

"And Then The Song"

"Kno ye thy path and follow of thy path true, for in this is thy deliverance. Now it is that ye shall be about the land and ye shall be about the land for purpose, for there shall be need of each of thee, and there shall be need of each spark of the Light, each point of the star, each glimmer, yea there is need of thee. For ye ones shall be the light in the darkness and ye shall gather about thee those that do cry in their confusion to be lifted. And ye shall give to these ones nourishment and ye shall give to these ones sustenance that they might be calmed, that they might partake of the Word, that they might be ready to be lifted. This do I ask of thee, ye ones who do follow after me, this do I ask of thee. Kno ye I shall abide with thee and I shall minister through thee, one to another. As ye hold forth thy hand, so shall it be as I hold forth mind hand, and yea as ye hold forth your hand, so shall it be that ye hold forth thine hand to me. Know this be so, and so be it, as it is given to thee.

Now the tears shall wash of the land and then the song, the smile of the heavens shall dry the tears of the Earth and the skies shall be as new. And the soil shall be fertile and shall be new. And there shall be rivers and there shall be waters that ye kno not of. And it shall be as has been told, as has been foretold, for the hour has come when all shall be, as has been given to thee. Kno this.

Think ye not I spout in folly. Think ye not I spout of a different day, one of many many sleeps from now. No, I speak of the morrow, for the hour has passed when we shall speak of the distant day. Kno ye this day approaches, the day is with thee. Kno this be so as has been given thee. Kno this be so. Now be ye as ones to know of thy preparation and be ye as ones ready for what comes to thee, for in thy testing shall be thy preparation for the hour that shall begin the new. I am thine Edler Brother who does speak. I am He who didst walk this Earth as Jesus.

I am He that is known as **Esu, Sananda.**

I am known to thee as the Christed One.

Blessings to thee, peace to thee."

Selah di dak di eno cum eta

Recorded by Tuieta

"We Will See, O' Ones of Light"

"Ye ones who have walked of the Light, have not touched ones who you will learn to call brother. For the hour approaches when ones shall cum to your door, and they shall be as absolute strangers to your outward eye. And yet they shall ask to enter. For they will be ones that have not home, not bread, not cloth upon their backs. And they will be scarred. And they will be dirty. And they will knock upon your door, and they will ask to enter. And this shall be your test, O' ones of Light. This shall be your test. Would you bid these ones enter?

As you sit in your comfort and your security, you eagerly do say, 'Oh yes Lord, I will bid these ones enter. And I will share my bed with them. And I will give them clothing. And I will feed them.' And I say, we will see. We will see, o' ones of Light."

Received by Tuieta   **—Theoaphylos**

"Ye Are Divine In Thine Origin"

"Behold Me—see Mine hand move, for am I not there, am I not within the manifestation, am I not the unmanifest, am I not the ever-present all powerful—Omnipotent Father which has given unto thee being? Were it not so, thou wouldst not be—for from Me hast thou gone forth as a perfect being. While I say unto thee: Thou has divided thineself many times, yet I say unto thee: Thou shall return unto Me made Whole and perfect, even as thou went out. For this do I say unto thee: Give thanks it is now come when thine days of wandering in darkness shall end, and it shall be a glorious end—for end it shall, and it shall end in thine Victory, for has it not been foretold thee? I say: Ye shall return unto Me the Victor. While I say: 'Thine waiting hast been long and hard,' I say: It shall end victoriously. Arise Mine Children, Come, sing ye praise, the

day of thine deliverance is come—sing ye praise it is done. I say unto thee: Give unto thineself credit for being Mine blessed Children—for have I not given unto thee of Mineself that ye might be called Mine Children? The Sons of God art thou—I say ye are divine in thine origin, and ye shall not forget this, for I say unto thee: It is the way of man to forget his Origin; too I say: Ye shall remember it, for One shall touch thee, and thine memory shall be restored unto thee, for I have willed it so—so let it be for

                                    —I AM thine
Recorded by Sister Thedra   **—Father, Solen Aum Solen**

"Lift Up Your Voice In Song—
Hear The Song of the Heavens"

"*Rejoice! Rejoice! Rejoice ye ones of Israel.* Hear ye our words. Feel our thots. Receive that which we do share with thee. For though we are the seven we speak as the voice of one, for we are the *Archangels* that do watch over, that do guide the hand that cums to ones of Earth. Lift up your voice in song. Lift your heart in prayerful thanksgiving. Receive of the newness that cums and rejoice in thy receiving. Open thy hearts that the blessings and the bounty might pour forth to one and all. Receive and rejoice as ye receive. Be ye as ones to look about and see of the newness of the season. See of the birthing. And feel of the awakening.

And as ye do give of thine all so do ye receive of All. For that which is thine is only a portion. And as ye do surrender of thine portion so do ye make thy self ready to receive of the Total, to receive of the All. O' ye ones, ye small ones of Terra, see thy plight, see what ye have done. And be ye as ones to cast from thy selves thy error and thy foolish ways. And be as

ones to surrender to thine Divine Creator. And in thy surrender is thy rejoicing. And in thy surrender shall ye hear the song of the heavens. And in they surrender shall ye be clothed in Light. *Rejoice ! Rejoice! Rejoice! Rejoice! Rejoice! Rejoice! Rejoice!* For as each does speak so are the blessings of thy Father Yahweh rained upon thee. Bow thee thy knee before the Creator that ye might be as one to receive thy blessing. And yea, we do speak as one voice, but we are the voice of the seven. For we are the Archangels that do bend our knee that we might be close to ye ones of Terra. Selah Selah Selah"
—Uriel, Gabriel, Zadkiel, Raphael, Michael, Jophiel & Chamuel
Received by Tuieta

EPILOGUE

CHANGING PATTERNS,

WHAT IS THE SOURCE,
THE VOICE OF ALL

THE

W ONE N

PHOTO BY MICHAEL ZANGER

"This Is An Important Doorway"

"For Those That Understand The Kingdom Of The Air"

"A teacher who is willing now to learning ways beyond the usual path. A teacher that is to teach your conscious mind, this is a teacher that is a bridge of energy. We do not conceptualize the things you would call matter or objects, except as the vibration. As this particular vibration takes its form as a bridging between higher soul energy and the way in which individuals who are communicating by such energy— reach your conscious mind in one way or another. A process therefore called channelling. The way this is, often occurs and is accelerated when *you are able to make a shift, you are able to change your point of view.*

"Time to be shifted so that each one of you are your own best disciple and guru and you are the ones who learn from this and that you do not place it on an outside being. So then you will understand as you experiment, let us say, with some of these shifting patterns for yourselves.

One of these important things to recognize is simply that of the north American native people, and especially of the energies understood there by the four elements.

In each of these elements you have many symbols for yourselves and in those of you understanding the *air* you will see as well that your perception and your clarity will also, be affected by the symbols that you receive as you view the air with longing, with beauty, with emotion, and spiritual eyes. In other words if what you are seeing when you look into a changing cloud pattern is a thing that affects you into wonderment, then think of the source of such, *no* do not ask, simply create, or even you might use this foolish word, *guess!* what the source *is!* Then in that moment in which you see it as it might be, imagine inside praise for that source. In other words, the air has a sound, or perhaps it is for you a conceptualization of *change,* or you see it suddenly in your life or in a past life as a change, as you have perceived it and understood it. In that moment praise those sources by which this came. This is an important doorway for those that understand the kingdom of the air.

There are many beings there who do not understand about some of the most basic tenants of coming into incarnation, which is the simple process of *being,* this itself that they do not understand.

We have spoken extensively about *earth* in the past. It is a very important element at this time in particular because the Earth is learning so much right now from each of you. Hopefully it is learning a lot about *love,* about a *hope* for a peaceful planet. If this is what you wish to teach this Earth, know that she will receive this from you. It is also highly likely in the *coming change* time that the energies of the beings who live within the Earth may be revealed more clearly to mankind. This in itself may upset the equilibrium balance of the powers that be on this planet. Because what will be glimpsed will be a great new source of energy, of power, of ways to understand things and all of the rest of it. And in the struggle to work with this sort of thing there may be entirely new shifts. You have already seen how much the Earth herself affects all of humanity with the precious nature of oil that is held within her body. So can this occur again and again in many other ways, as various things are discovered within her.

Regarding the element of *fire,* this of course symbolized for mankind now by the nuclear arsenals, and at the same time within every human heart the ability to let these fires be fanned to the place where; either they are put out by starvation—there is no one left interested in building such weapons—or, they are fanned to the point where those involved see at last the tremendous quest for power, the fear they have inside and the difficulties they have struggled with.

And lastly of course the element of *water,* and this is of

great importance right now. For many of you have had this emotion, this sense inside of what could be in this time; things unachieved but also the sense inside of a love uncommunicated —thus the emotional body begins to take on all the trappings that tell you somehow inside that you do not deserve love because you have not shared it enough, because you do not understand it enough, or whatever your own pattern is. The truth of course, as we shake off these patterns, is that you understand love and you are willing to share it in the world. And this is a simple solution also to these things of the gentle depression, or reduced activity, or listlessness that many feel at this time of the year. It is not simply because of the reduced exposure of the sun, this is an important symbol, but it is also this emotional business. And so for some of you it is only necessary to think of someone you have loved dearly in the past and then magnify this energy and then pour it to someone who might need your love right now! This is difficult to do if your conscious mind revolves around and around with the older pattern, of non-deserving or things that do not permit you to accept of this love as being capable of being projected through your *being*. Yet if you could but see through the eyes of your guides, you would see in a moment the light of the strength that pours from your heart at the very moment you begin such a meditation, or such a thought.

Now of course each of these symbols are important for all mankind in many other ways. It is likely for those who can see into such realms, a little bit about the process of transformation from various dimensional realities that are more easily shall we say, conformed to make the space travel easier—that of the understanding of the kingdom of the air as a medium for transformation will be recognized. It is also an inherent thing in such a process of transformation that these beings, the kingdom of the air, are in some way given a little bit of strength, happiness, change—they are not left hurt. Now this is what often happens in the combustion engines of rockets.

The beings who co-inhabit this planet with you do not like very much to have their immediate locale burst into very hot flame if you might imagine. And so then, those ways of transformation that are not just gentle, but allow the kingdom of the air to be made a little happy, given a little inspiration, a little bit of enlightening energy. This is one of the secrets of space travel and one of the things that is not yet understood by those who study things strictly from the point of view of their use as limited weapons.

Now what you may notice for yourselves then, as these cloud formations begin to coalesce and change, that there is a happiness, there is an energy, there is a projection. This is fine, it is interesting to observe it, and so on, but as we have often spoken* in the past of techniques by which you may see the kingdoms of the air more clearly. Why not participate in such a transformation, so you may understand it more yourself. Yet these can be explained by the use of inert gas technologies combined with various crystalline formations in interesting geometric configurations.

And of course we are not permitted to give this at the present time because humanity might even as yet use these things as weapons. But you may even understand these yourselves.

And so as you witness these changes, think of the kingdom of the air. Think of beings that wish to understand the very essence of *being*, no they are not struggling with breath or food, or some of the activities of relationship or change, or time even, but they are struggling with the inner concept of coming into existence. Something you perhaps take for granted. Love them for this. Let your love pour into that cloud area, but not to love the space beings who may be using this as a transformation point, but to love these beings

(* the book *Other Kingdoms)*

who assist them unknowingly perhaps, for what is knowledge to one who has not even created form?! But as they are welcomed, you welcome them, and say unto these beings, 'existence has its benefits, existence is filled with love, feel my love for you in your willingness to take of this.' This may yield to your etheric sight many interesting new things. These are important techniques to be understood in the coming years."
Channeled by Jon Fox **—Hilarion**

"No One Knows What Is Beyond The Door Until They Open It Up"

"Whatever you do, do it to the grandest of the Lord God of your Being. Bless your intelligence, bless your hands, bless the door that you labor behind. *Bless everything—you are a God.* When that aura of understanding changes, you are expanding. And the greater the attitude the greater the knowingness. The more that you know, the greater the doors that open to you. Why that is illustrated by doors by this that I AM?, because no one knows what is beyond the door until they open it up and walk through it. If opportunity comes to you it comes in the sign of a door. And it says:

'OPPORTUNITY'

It is a dream you have manifested, you have earned the doors. Now, you say 'But if I only knew what was behind it. But socially conditioned entities never go beyond the door because they are suspicious and afraid of the unknown. Know why?, it means they have to be different. And indeed masters, they have to approach something and make something of it themselves.

The door is a thought. The *key* that opens the door is *God. What lies beyond the door is wisdom.* Wisdom that you have never gained before. If it was already there the door wouldn't be there. Doors do not open to stagnation or social consciousness, they are just not there, you see?, because they know they are not there, *you understand?*

The unfolding master's adventures begin to intensify. Everything that he begins to unfold—and open up here—and this God can become one with—takes you rapidly from the past and present onward. Opportunity as it is so termed and understood by you is unlimited and the door will just fit you. The room beyond is just large enough for that little unlimited understanding you allowed to come through, it facilitates it nicely. And the more you endeavor, and embark and expand, the greater the rooms become. And one day there will be a different door open to you, and beyond that door is beyond time. This lifetime is to be *loved. It is life, it is God.* Whatever you do, *embrace it, allow,* don't compare it to anyone else. Support your knowingness, be unlimited in that devotion. Be unlimited to you. And you can be anything there is to be and still be God."
Channeled by J.Z. Knight **—Ramtha**

"I AM The Voice That Speaks
As The Combination Of All Ones"

"Beloved Brothers and Sisters of Planet Earth:

As you have partaken of our banquet, may you find that which will begin to wet your appetite. It is hoped that the hunger that is deep withIN you is stirred to give sustenance to *all ones* that desire to grow in their awareness and their *AT-One-Ment* with the *creative force. We* have revealed ourselves to you both visually and through the written Word. Know that We *do* exist and are constantly with you, and all *ones* that would receive *us.* We do not come to trespass of your own free will but we come to *assist* you in your conscious evolvement.

The end of the cycle is with you for all *ones* of planet Earth. You will not, by the hand of the creative force, be allowed to wallow in your present state. That which you have created of pain and suffering is to be taken from you and from Planet Earth. You shall have the *opportunity* to come into the *light* or again assume habitation in a situation that is comparable to that one which you know on Earth.

THE CHOICE IS YOUR OWN ALONE.

In this small book we have attempted to stimulate that portion of you which would cause you to desire only that which is of the *highest order.* The photographs have demonstrated *our* vehicles and *our ever presence.* The Words that have come forth speak to you in the Universal language of *love* and *peace.* Know we *are* the *guardians* of the *skies.* We *are* your Brothers of the ethers. We *are* of this Universe and those Universes and Galaxies that are as yet unknown to you. We *are one* with you in the creative force. Know as you observe *us* that *we* come in Peace, *We* come in *love, We* come in *universal brotherhood.*

I AM the Voice that speaks as the combination of All Ones that have presented to you in this Book.

—I AM the Voice of the **Ashtar Command**
SALU!"

Received by Tuieta

PHOTO BY KEVIN LAHEY